DELTA TEACHER DEVELOPMENT S
Series editors Mike Burghall and Lindsay Clandfield

# The Company Words Keep

Lexical chunks in language teaching

Paul Davis and Hanna Kryszewska

Published by
DELTA PUBLISHING
Quince Cottage
Hoe Lane
Peaslake
Surrey GU5 9SW
England

www.deltapublishing.co.uk

© Delta Publishing 2012

First published 2012
Reprinted 2013

ISBN 978-1-905085-20-0

All rights reserved. No part of this publication may be reproduced, stored in a retrieval system or transmitted in any form or by any means, electronic, mechanical, photocopying, recording or otherwise, without the prior permission of the publishers.

Edited by Mike Burghall
Designed by Christine Cox
Cover photo © iStockphoto.com/Dominic Course
Back cover photos by Jim Wright
Printed in China by RR Donnelley

To **Mario Rinvolucri**, our friend, whose books have edged ELT forward, and whose presence has always given us a push.

Hania and Paul

## Acknowledgements

Very special thanks to:

Mike Burghall, our editor, who contributed so much.

Nick Boisseau and Lindsay Clandfield for your belief in us.

Christine Cox for giving the book such a user-friendly shape.

Many thanks to the key figures in the field, from whose inspiring lectures and seminars we have benefited immensely:

Ron Carter, Michael Hoey, Michael Lewis, Mike McCarthy, Michael Rundell.

# From the authors

My adventure with chunks started in the mid-nineties after I heard Michael Lewis give a presentation at IATEFL Poland.

Michael introduced the concept of chunking and, at the same time, admitted that although there was a new linguistic description of the language there did not seem any new methodology springing from this description.

A few years later, together with Paul, we started thinking about writing a resource book, voicing a question that we found crucial and to which we are beginning to find an answer:

> *Does a new language description have to result in new methodology?*

Despite the fact that chunks and corpus analysis have been with us well over two decades, there has been no major breakthrough in teaching. Linguistics provides the data and we teachers recognise the interesting facts that are revealed about language, yet we see hardly any way we can implement these findings.

I am a non-native speaker of English. English is a foreign language to me and I learned it with the help of teachers who believed that if we amassed a lot of new words and mastered the intricacies of English grammar we would speak perfect English.

Subsequent contact with non-native speakers who had *acquired* the language rather than *learned* it taught me something new. I often spoke 'in English' but didn't speak 'English'. I could communicate, but the language I produced was less real and less right.

Later in my adult life I had to learn a lot of chunks or 'routines', and I find I am still learning them. I feel I have wasted a lot of time.

As a teacher, I want to help my students to learn about and use chunks as early as possible. By doing so in a conscious and planned way, I can introduce an element of *acquisition* into the process of *learning* a language. It is what I would call 'conscious acquisition'.

Teaching my students to learn chunks is a way of improving my teaching – and not just part of an academic debate.

I had seen presentations and read about lexical chunking, but what really got me going was noticing the students naturally using chunks in lower-level classes I taught.

In a standard first lesson with my beginners, I presented *'What's your name?'* and *'I'm Paul'*. Then the students milled around with a piece of paper, using the language to make a list of names. So far so good. But many got bored with the repetition and shortened it to *'You?'* or *'And you?'*

My students were chunking down – naturally. I thought about getting them to say the full sentence; then I thought about it again and let it go: they were doing what they would do in their mother tongue and what native speakers would do in English.

> *Why sacrifice this natural spoken English for a bit of grammar practice?*

Later, I realised that I instinctively did the same myself. I didn't ask *'Did you have a nice weekend?'* I would say *'Nice weekend?'* And they would reply in chunks: *'Yeah, grandma's house'*. Brief conversations which were low on grammar but dense with chunks – and great confidence builders.

I was struck by a comment of a friend of mine (Simon Marshall) about talking to an advanced non-native speaker of English he met. He said he complemented them, after a few minutes, saying how good their English was but, after a few more minutes, he regretted saying it.

I think Simon meant that they were overusing their knowledge of grammar and words and so the conversation became boring. As David Brazil puts it: making a speech rather than speaking.

So an early exposure to the idea of lexical chunking can have long-term benefits as the student becomes more proficient. And not just speaking, but writing too. I noticed that most of the lexical mistakes of my advanced students were not so much that they use the wrong word than that they use the wrong combinations.

I put this down to the fact that they have learnt single words early in their language learning – rather than chunks.

# Contents

| | |
|---|---|
| From the authors | Page 3 |

## Part A — Page 7
Glossary of terms — Page 21

## Part B — Page 25

### 1  In the beginning — Page 27

**Learner awareness**

| | |
|---|---|
| A first lesson | Page 27 |
| Real classroom routines | Page 28 |
| Chunks in your head | Page 28 |
| Answers to questions | Page 29 |
| 'Brain sludge' | Page 29 |
| How many words? | Page 30 |
| International words | Page 31 |
| One-word conversations | Page 31 |
| Three or five … or more | Page 32 |
| Listening for chunks | Page 33 |
| Reading for chunks | Page 33 |
| Pass the chunk | Page 34 |
| Chunking around a word | Page 34 |
| Nice and easy | Page 35 |
| Chunking around a theme | Page 36 |
| Chunks in the picture | Page 37 |

**Learner training**

| | |
|---|---|
| Get this! | Page 37 |
| Be a sport | Page 38 |
| Urban dictionary online | Page 39 |
| Translate that! | Page 40 |
| Bilingual dictionaries online | Page 41 |
| Vocabulary lists | Page 41 |
| A class concordance | Page 42 |
| Learner concordances | Page 42 |

### 2  In the coursebook — Page 43

**Games**

| | |
|---|---|
| Draw a chunk | Page 43 |
| A chunky board game | Page 44 |
| Mime a chunk | Page 44 |

**Dialogues and texts**

| | |
|---|---|
| Recycling a dialogue | Page 45 |
| Conversational manoeuvres | Page 45 |
| Reduction | Page 46 |
| Expansion | Page 46 |
| Shadow thinking | Page 47 |
| Chunk for chunk | Page 48 |
| L1–L2 translation | Page 48 |
| Mischunking | Page 49 |

**Exercises and exams**

| | |
|---|---|
| Building around a chunk | Page 49 |
| Chunks first, then grammar | Page 50 |
| Everything is right | Page 51 |
| Tolerating ambiguity | Page 52 |
| A word or a phrase? | Page 52 |
| A test with a twist | Page 53 |
| Gaps with a twist | Page 53 |
| Gapped sentences DIY | Page 54 |

### 3  In action — Page 53

**Practice**

| | |
|---|---|
| The class blues | Page 55 |
| A 'likely' wife | Page 56 |
| Mind the gap | Page 57 |
| 7–1 dialogues | Page 57 |
| Dense dialogues | Page 58 |
| Conversation countdown | Page 58 |
| Incomplete grammar | Page 59 |
| Grammar from chunks | Page 60 |
| Creative chunks | Page 60 |
| Skilful monologue | Page 61 |
| Rapid repairs | Page 62 |

# Contents

Priming
- Small change, big difference — Page 62
- Restricted access — Page 63
- Grammar in chunks — Page 63

Pragmatics
- Real-life responses — Page 64
- Gossip, not communication — Page 65
- Fixed expression rituals — Page 65
- What was the question? — Page 66
- Old versus young — Page 66
- Colourful clichés — Page 67
- From culture to culture — Page 68

**4 In authentic contexts** — Page 69

The world we live in
- Cut it out! — Page 69
- Signs and notices — Page 70
- Going shopping — Page 70
- 'To do' lists — Page 71
- Textspeak — Page 71
- Advanced txtspk — Page 72

The words we live with
- Headline collage — Page 73
- Old words, new partnerships — Page 73
- Chunks in the news — Page 74
- Speculative summaries — Page 74
- Twisted chunks — Page 75
- Howzaboutit? — Page 76
- Chunks in novels — Page 76
- Literature through textspeak — Page 77
- Kiss the sky — Page 78
- Songs in your head — Page 79
- Song titles (and brackets) — Page 79
- Film titles — Page 80
- Chunk in cheek — Page 80
- From English to L1 — Page 81
- From L1 to English — Page 81

**5 In data** — Page 82

Very high frequency
- Chunk champion — Page 82
- Chunk quest — Page 83
- Fight it out! — Page 83
- Fight for culture — Page 84
- Chunk Bingo — Page 85
- Top 20 words — Page 86
- Top 100 collocations — Page 87
- Opinion versus data — Page 87

Very good company
- Complete the collocation — Page 88
- Friendly facilities — Page 89
- Google the chunk — Page 90
- From chunks to sentences — Page 90
- Going for a song — Page 91
- The tip of the iceberg — Page 92
- Dictionary versus dictionary — Page 93
- Picture this! — Page 93
- Picture dictionaries online — Page 94
- Word sketch — Page 95
- Your last chance — Page 96
- Questions, queries and quibbles — Page 97

**Part C** — Page 101

- Review — Page 102
- Reflect on your lessons — Page 104
- Reflect on your learners — Page 108
- Research
  - The Web — Page 115
  - Bibliography — Page 117

From the editors — Page 119
From the publisher — Page 120

There are three key developments in the history of chunks: one in the thirteenth century and two in the middle part of the last century.

**1230 AD onwards:** interest in concordances of a corpus

The text of the Latin Bible was the first corpus, and the first concordance was done by a Dominican friar called Hugo of St-Cler in 1230. The purpose was to access efficiently the frequently-used text. Later concordances were made for the Bible in the vernacular and for Shakespeare.

There were attempts in both Britain and America in the early twentieth century to compile a corpus and concordances for general English, but these were hampered by a lack of resources available before the advent of cheap computational power – Hugo was said to have 500 monks working on his concordance of the Bible corpus!

**1920s onwards:** increasing interest in word partnerships by linguists

Interest in word partnerships is generally attributed to J R Firth who, from the 1920s to his death in the 1960s, challenged the orthodoxy and stressed the importance of collocations and word partnerships – *'You shall know a word by the company it keeps'*.

**1930/40s onwards:** development of the electronic computer

Alan Turing is generally recognised as the developer of the modern electronic computer in the 1940s. Later, when computers became cheap enough to use for general rather than military use, they were applied to language and corpora were developed.

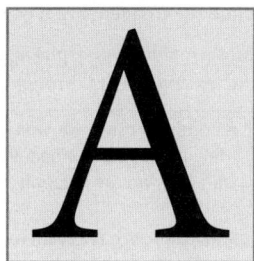

*'You shall know a word by the company it keeps.'*
John Rupert Firth

▶ For early practice on the intuitive use of chunks, see the activity *A first lesson* on page 27.

▶ The Pathways, as suggested in Part A, indicate just a few of the connections between these pages and the rest of *The Company Words Keep*.

**The company words keep.** Not grammar. Not words. Word partnerships. Lexical density. Fixed expressions. Bits and pieces. Chunks.

These examples show that it is perfectly possible (and *usual* in spoken English) to express a message with lexical chunks rather than full grammatical sentences. If you know a few chunks in a language – *a pint of Guinness, a skinny latte, a packet of crisps* – you are likely to get a result (a smile will help, too!). The polite forms of grammar such as *Can I have …? Could I have …? Give me a …* will get you no result on their own – unless you are good at pointing. Language learners seem to know this intuitively and so are generally more interested in lexis. Learners will often buy both a dictionary and a grammar book. But it is the dictionary they have in their bag – and the grammar book they leave at home.

This is true for native speakers just as much as it is for language learners; chunks relieve cognitive effort and increase naturalness. Native speakers become less fluent if they are talking about a subject area they are unfamiliar with, because they do not have their chunks 'ready prepared'. It seems we retrieve a chunk first and add the grammar second – the exact opposite of most coursebooks and syllabuses, which have the grammatical structure first and then add the lexis.

When non-natives have not experienced the chunk, they often construct sound grammatical sentences. Someone who has not come across, say, *'By the way'* might construct *'There is something that I need to tell you'* or *'Another subject is …'*. Good thinking, good grammar, intelligent guesses – but very *unlikely* utterances, which need to be interpreted by the listener. It is probably easier to use the grammar structures if one has chunks readily to hand.

## Three factors

However, the fact that chunking and the Lexical Approach have become 'buzz words' is not because of intuition. It is because of the research that has been done over the last decades in the universities.

Corpus linguistics has provided a new description of language, shown the importance of chunks to well-formed language and led to a shift away from early Chomskian ideas of deep structure and of performance and competence. It shows that we store language in ready-made chunks that are retrieved and used – rather than elaborately constructing grammar each time we speak.

If we know the chunks associated with a particular area, we are fluent and articulate in that area; if we do not, we stumble and are relatively inarticulate, because we have to try laboriously to construct the language.

▶ You will find more on modern tools which help to explore chunks in activities in Chapter Five, and in the 'Research' section in Part C.

The research that is being done is based on the coming together of three factors:
1 the use of corpus data
2 an increased interest by linguists in word partnerships
3 the availability of cheap computational tools that can sort the data with ease and show the environment and the frequency of a word

Word partnerships provided by corpus analysis of the language are often explored by grammarians and lexicographers through concordances like the one below.

> e concrete road. He was in a <u>dream</u>, aware of the sh
> t few days had seemed like a <u>dream</u>, but now, with th
> with a start as though his <u>dream</u> had frightened

However, such concordances have relatively little appeal to learners, although this may be because they are not *used to* them, even though there have been some attempts to use them in class for learner training and developing language awareness bu building language activities around concordances. And there are activities in this book which give the learners a chance to be introduced to them in a more formal setting, build their own simple concordances and take control of the process.

Using concordances like the one illustrated above, linguists have described different types of chunks. The terms 'word' and 'vocabulary' are being replaced with the term 'chunk' and 'lexis' in English Language Teaching. A chunk can refer to many things: a single word, a collocation (now usually referred to as a 'word partnership') or a fixed expression (which, as its name suggests, is fixed, and includes idioms and can even be a whole sentence of fixed type – called a 'routine').

▶ Full details of the references quoted in Part A are given in the 'Research' bibliography on page 117.

So the coming together of our three factors has led to the present interest in a more lexical approach in ELT. John Sinclair (1991) provided a framework for use of the corpus, and the first one to have any real impact on ELT was the Cobuild project at Birmingham University, UK, which was developed in the early 1980s and resulted in the first corpus-based dictionary (*Collins Cobuild*, 1987) and, in 1988/9, a coursebook (*Collins Cobuild Course* – still worth a look if you can find a copy). This early work by John Sinclair had been built on by James R Nattinger and Jeanette S DeCarrico, Michael Lewis, Dave and Jane Willis, Michael Hoey, Michael Rundell, and Roland Carter and Michael McCarthy, amongst others.

▶ For how to explore the corpus as a body of language see *Fight it out!* on page 83 and *Opinion versus data* on page 87.

Corpus-based linguistics provides raw data. This means that our view of language and what to teach can now be based on interpretation of that data rather than expert intuition, as was previously the case. What computers are good at, of course, is counting and sorting. And so we can see the *frequency* and the *environment* of a word – and get insights into what is more useful to teach and the context in which to teach it.

Also, when one looks at the mass of corpus data, the prevalence of chunks is evident, and so we can suggest that it is a natural process to chunk and that a knowledge of chunks would speed up the language learning process, foster fluency and improve exam results. At the very least, if a learner learns a three-word chunk they not only learn the meaning of that particular chunk but they also build up knowledge of the individual words that make it up.

## Three questions

▶ The terminology we use is further developed in the 'Glossary of terms' on page 21 and then reviewed in Part C.

In this book we have usually used the relatively neutral word 'chunk' or the phrase 'word partnership'. We have avoided a variety of other terms such as collocation, colligation, fixed expression, unfixed expression, idiom, cliché – partly to keep it simple but also because these terms tend to be used in a technical way in linguistics and, as terms, they are often disputed or confused in the literature.

However, in *The Company Words Keep* these terms *are* used, hopefully with precision, when we think they are useful or enlightening. And we have provided a glossary of terms, some of which may be new to you, on page 21. This brings us to the first of three questions:

*'I have seen grown men fighting with broken bottles over whether 'donkey' meant the same thing as 'ass'.'*
Anthony Burgess

*'He uses statistics rather as a drunk uses a lamppost – for support rather than illustration.'*
Benjamin Disraeli.

## What is a chunk?

The quotes opposite are to the point. Language is very emotive, people write angrily to the newspapers about language. And linguists spend their careers and write theses and books defining this or that chunk. And they use statistics. And they do not agree with each other. And they fight. And they will continue to fight.

Luckily we do not need an exact definition; we need a working definition. It is clear that just as people have relationships – one-night stands, affairs, marriages, lifelong friendships – so do words. The relationship between people can be complicated, and so can the relationship between words. But, for our purposes, a chunk is a word partnership; two or more words that stand together, usually with a key word, and are primed to have a specific meaning. Form and meaning are one. A chunk is simply a meaningful bit of language. The word 'at' has no precise meaning on its own but it comes alive in chunks such as *not at all*, *at the table*, *at five*, *at times*.

Chunks are *'observable facts of usage'* (Sinclair). Corpus data or a good corpus-based dictionary will provide the 'meaning in use' of a specific chunk, as well as providing its environment and its frequency, as we have said. So our aim as teachers is to get our learners to develop their perceptions of the patterns; to observe and to note.

## How fixed is a chunk?

Chunks are fixed, then, but some chunks are fixed more than others:

- Some partnerships are very rigid: *golden handshake* is pretty fixed, at least in part because *golden* is a relatively rare word and is only used in a handful of chunks, and rarely used on its own to describe something. *Golden* and *handshake* have a strong likelihood of co-occurring and give a strong idiomatic meaning. These types of chunks are often referred to in the literature as 'fixed expressions' and include idioms, sayings or clichés.
- A *firm handshake* is less fixed, as there are other ways of describing a handshake and *firm* is used in lots of other contexts. *Firm* and *handshake* are likely to co-occur and have a specific meaning. These types of chunks are often referred to in the literature as 'word partnerships' or 'collocations'.
- *Another handshake* is pretty unfixed. It has meaning in a context, but *another* can be used in many other contexts. It's a perfectly acceptable combination but is neither common nor idiomatic. These types of chunks are often referred to in the literature as 'unfixed expressions'.

▶ For more on this issue, see the activity *Restricted access* on page 63.

## How long is a chunk?

It seems (George A Miller, 1956) that we are comfortable with retaining up to seven (plus or minus two) bits of information – we can retain telephone numbers because, excluding codes, they are this length. But not many people remember their credit card number. This is why it is split into groups of four on the card: so it can be chunked and said in chunks over the phone. Easy. There is a pattern which is observable and helpful.

▶ The issue of the length of chunks is dealt with in *A 'likely' wife* on page 56 – amongst other activities.

The number of syllables in the words in the chunk is also significant, since it seems it is easier to retain polysyllabic words than single syllable words. This means that the limit of a chunk such as *on top of the world*, which consists solely of monosyllabic words, is normally five. There are longer monosyllabic chunks, such as *keep right on to the end of the road* which seem to break the rule; but just like telephone numbers they can be broken down into patterns that are easier to retain: *keep right on / to the end of the road*.

We haven't found any evidence in the literature, but it seems also that prime numbers are favoured in monosyllabic chunks: so two, three, five, seven and nine is a tendency, whereas four and six and eight are rare. Counter-intuitively, chunks containing polysyllabic words seem easier to remember, and the limit for them is normally seven words but on occasion may be nine.

▶ For more on learner training and developing inner criteria see *Answers to a question* (page 29), *'Brain sludge'* (page 29) and *How many words?* (page 30).

There are, of course, other questions about chunks that need an answer:
- Where do they begin and end? And how do you recognise them?
- What restrictions are there? And do they have slots to fit in pronouns or other bits of language?

Rather than enter into too detailed a technical discussion, there are activities in this book which deal with these points through awareness-raising and encouraging learners (and teachers!) to develop their inner criteria.

# Chunks and language

*'Words — so innocent and powerless as they are, as standing in a dictionary, how potent for good and evil they become, in the hands of one who knows how to combine them.'*
Nathaniel Hawthorne

Why are chunks important to language and, therefore, language learning? Well, as J R Firth said: *'When in doubt go to the data'*. Even a superficial look at the evidence shows that no word is a hermit, all words are known by the company they keep. And it seems that chunks are about three times more prevalent in language than single words. A look at any good corpus-based dictionary will show that, while a headword will probably have a meaning or two when it stands alone, it will have entry after entry after entry in combination with other words to form a chunk.

And if you learn the chunks, you get a least a cursory understanding of the words too; learning a word in isolation invites errors, as learners use it in the wrong environment – they need to know what goes *around* the word to be able to produce it when speaking or writing. Also, 'recoding' is a powerful weapon for retention – if the learners get the habit of putting each encounter with a word into a chunk, then they are more likely to retain the information.

It seems, also, that chunking is a natural process. Learners do it in their native language and so, with a bit of awareness-raising in class, we can get them to transfer this skill to the target language. If they concentrate on learning chunks rather than words – especially if they are accustomed to doing this from beginners' level – they will become more efficient learners.

*'The most valuable of all talents is that of never using two words when one will do.'*
Thomas Jefferson

**Single words** Words are chunks too. If we define a lexical chunk as a 'sanctioned unit of meaning', then words standing alone fit the definition. If you stand in the street and shout *Taxi* it has an agreed meaning. If you exclaim *pathetic*, then this also has an agreed meaning: that you are not in agreement with a statement or an action. It's worth noting here that, although words obviously do have meaning when spoken in isolation, we use only some thousands – whereas in partnership with other words to make chunks, we have tens of thousands primed and ready to use.

**Word partnerships** Word partnership is a term which is now used more than collocation. It describes words which we are likely to store together for use to make an agreed meaning. So *pathetic creature* is a likely combination to insult someone; *pathetic animal* is an unlikely utterance as an insult. *Don't be so pathetic* is a likely combination; *Please be less pathetic*, while being technically correct, is an unlikely combination.

*'The meaning of a word is its use in the language.'*
Ludwig Wittgenstein

**Colligation** Word partnerships/collocations are combinations of words to form a chunk with a specific meaning. They are typically *adjective + noun, adjective + noun + adverb*, and … ; well, there are lots of combinations. The company a word keeps! Colligation is, according to Michael Hoey, 'the *grammatical* company words keep' – a word partnership that involves an element of grammar to give a specific meaning. An example he gives is 'not surprising'. We don't 'negate' other similar words to make a chunk – *not amazing* or *not astonishing* are unlikely combinations. But *surprising* is a strong match with a bit of grammar: 'not'.

**Fixed expressions** Whereas word partnerships or collocations are a relatively loose combination of words, some chunks are more fixed. The term 'fixed expression' is generally used to describe idioms, clichés and sayings. But it also includes more useful functional chunks, such as *by the way* and *happy birthday*. Fixed expressions have become the standard way of expressing a specific meaning and are used as part of a sentence. They are fixed in form and meaning and are restricted in their use so that, for example, it's fine to give advice by saying *No use crying over spilt milk* or *Don't cry over spilt milk*, but unlikely you will say *I'm always crying over split milk* or *You are going to be crying over spilt milk*. It's fine to say *he/she/you think(s) a lot of him/her/yourself*, but the expression is restricted to commenting on others: *I think a lot of myself* is a very unlikely utterance.

**Routines** There are two kinds of chunks in this group, according to Michael Lewis (1993). The first are what can be called institutionalised expressions. They usually constitute a significant part of a sentence – opening it, or the first half: eg *What I wanted to say is …* or *In my opinion …* . They can also be a sentence in their own right – but where the grammar component is minimalised: eg *Not yet …, Good riddance! Same here*, etc.

▶ For an activity on routines, see *Translate that!* on page 40.

The second kind are archetypal utterances, which are a 'whole' and they follow grammar rules: eg *That does the trick! Easy does it, Do your duty!* Both are vital for fast, fluent delivery and have a pragmatic meaning, as we shall see. They lubricate spoken English and make the non-native sound more natural.

## Chunks in use

**Priming** This term has been put forward by Michael Hoey (2005) to describe the process by which a specific word or chunk comes to be loaded with a specific meaning as it is repeatedly encountered. The meaning is also tied to the context in which it is used. He gives an example for the genre of medical language: *a drinking problem* is something that an alcoholic would have, *a problem drinking* means a very sore throat or blockage. These chunks come ready primed with the meaning. The primings of a chunk closely fit that of the speech community in which the learner has learned the language. Although chunks are primed to have a use, the normal rules are there to be 'played about with'.

▶ For three activities on 'priming' see pages 62 and 63.

**Twisted clichés** We have said above that *golden handshake* is fixed and has a strong idiomatic meaning. Because it is rigidly fixed there is fun to be had, and shock value, in playing around with it. So if the amount of money is not terribly large, we could 'twist' it to *silver handshake* to make fun of the situation. *Golden handcuffs* is another twist of the cliché – where someone is tied by a large amount of money to a contract or agreement.

▶ Go to *Colourful clichés* on page 67.

Some chunks are very common – but tend to be relatively under-taught and to be under-used by learners. Some are very rare – but often taught and known and used by learners. However, the rare chunks, although not much used by native speakers, do have a role in ritual language exchanges and in language play. Contrast the following two lists of chunks:

| 1 | 2 |
|---|---|
| talking about | It's raining cats and dogs |
| at the moment | It's a funny old world |
| it seems | There's nowt so queer as folk |
| over there | Who would have thought it? |
| hang on | He thinks he's the cat's whiskers |
| come on | Gone to meet his maker |
| I suppose | A good time was had by all |

If you google the British National Corpus and do a simple search, you can type any of the chunks above and get the frequency. When we did the first two in each list, we found this:

- The chunks in the first list have a very high frequency (they all feature in the top 100 most frequent in the BNC and are therefore all highly 'teachable'). *Talking about* occurred 5,385 times, and *at the moment* 5,114.
- The chunks in the second list have a very low frequency. *Raining cats and dogs* had only two examples in the corpus and *funny old world* only 16.

▶ You can find out more in 'Research' in Part C, and *Question, queries and quibbles* (page 97) is dedicated to the BNC.

This raises the question of why native speakers store chunks such as *raining cats and dogs* and *it's a funny old world* – if we don't really use them. Carter and McCarthy suggest that some chunks, while being known to everybody, are used just once every seven years on average. We can offer two explanations:

> *Fixed expression rituals* on page 65 explores such scenarios.

**Pragmatic bonding rituals** Three people are sitting in a pub. There is a pause in the conversation as they finish ruining someone's reputation and the drinks are low. One person says: *Who would have thought it?*; the second: *There's nowt so queer as folk*; the third: *It's a funny old world, isn't it?* This exchange of clichés has two functions. Firstly it's a bonding ritual (these kinds of colourful clichés are often age-, culture- and gender-related). But it is also a pragmatic signal – *Do we three stay and have another drink and ruin someone else's reputation, or do we go home?* Some fixed expressions have a pragmatic meaning – they're not much used in 'open' speech.

**Language play** *It's raining cats and dogs* is normally known by language learners. But the evidence suggests it is not used by native speakers: there are very few occurrences in the British National Corpus. Why, then, do all native speakers have it stored as 'brain sludge'. One answer is that it is there to 'twist'. So if it is raining lightly, native speakers have been known to say *'it's raining kittens and puppies'*. Another example is an umbrella which has pictures of cats and dogs on it. A whole lot of language is there not to be used 'straight' – but to be played around with in conversation or in literature. Children also twist and play with language chunks as a learning aid: *What do you call a dinosaur with no eyes? D'yathinkhesaurus.*

> For more on playing with language and authentic contexts, see Chapter Four in particular.

While there is nothing wrong with *knowing* 'colourful' chunks, *using* them is problematic for non-natives. They would need a lot of them – a learner with a few chunks is an *'accident waiting to happen'* and, unless the learner has awareness of pragmatic meaning in bonding rituals or can twist meaning, they should, as the saying goes, 'avoid clichés like the plague'. It may be more useful for learners to concentrate on more frequent chunks like *'By the way'*!

### Chunks in the world

**Ownership** English is *the* international language, especially on the Web. The linguist David Crystal has put forward the view that everybody needs to function in three languages:

- their *home* language or dialect
- the accepted *educated* national language for their country
- *international* English

British English and American are just *two* of many varieties of English around the world. It is also a second language for more people than it is a first language, and many exchanges in English don't involve native speakers. The ownership of English by native speakers is being eroded. As a lingua franca, English is the property of all those who use the language in their own way and make contributions to it. In fact, native speakers can be more of a hindrance than a help. Just as non-natives probably need to learn international English, native speakers need to learn to speak international English too.

There is now research into how particular nationalities speak English, what their grammatical and lexical preferences are; one example of many is VOICE (Vienna-Oxford International Corpus of English) researching how Austrians speak English. This type of research can look at obvious problems – such as false friends and word-for-word translation – and also analyse the social and psychological background when a specific group use English as a 'lingua franca'.

> Key terms like *idiolect* are defined in the 'Glossary of terms' on page 21.

Our learners have to work out 'what is what' from among all the input they get – and develop their own 'idiolect'. They need to develop an awareness of whether the English chunks they see or hear in the local media, in their local shopping mall and in their own language are international. They need to be able to decide which chunks they meet internationally fit into their desired idiolect. Which is preferred: *cell* or *mobile*?

**Authenticity** If English is an international language, then chunks, by their nature, are everywhere in the environment and the media all over the world: so the use of authentic sources with our learners for awareness-raising is a feasible strategy. Getting learners to recognise chunks in their environment and in their leisure activities is a good start. Sources of authentic text are on products, in advertising – a trip around a kitchen or bathroom, or

> Chapter Four is dedicated to the use of chunks in authentic contexts.

▶ See the first the first activities in Chapter Four.

looking out of the bus window, will in most countries reveal a variety of chunks.

And the various media which are now internationally available over the Web can provide lots of listening and reading activities in which to spot the chunks. One of our favourites at the moment is the one-minute news on the BBC website. Play it two or three times on demand and set a simple task – the learners have to notice the subject and place and people involved in each story and then note down any chunks they have noticed and found interesting in each story. They pool the chunks and check the meaning together if necessary. Simple, authentic and to the point. It takes a few minutes of a lesson, but is repeatable, and learners quickly become more proficient and have a real sense of progress.

Our aim is to build and build our learners' awareness of chunks; to notice them in text and in real life. Then when speaking and writing – in class, in their jobs, in their social life and in exams – they will have the resource to retrieve ready-made chunks and develop a fluency.

**Idiomaticity** As chunks are used more and more, they often take on a meaning of their own.

| ONE HOUR PHOTOS | OPEN 24 HOURS A DAY | BARGAIN BASEMENT |
| READY IN 20 MINUTES | (Except 2am–8am) | UPSTAIRS |

In these notices, the chunk *one hour* is primed to mean 'quick', *24 hours a day* means 'most of the time' and *bargain basement* means 'cheap section of the store'. Not to be taken literally!

Things *wash up on the beach*, *we wash up after dinner* and someone who is no longer any good is *all washed up*. It is not just non-natives who might have difficulties here, children learning their first language have problems too, and it is the downfall of many a professional translator or interpreter.

And there are other cultural considerations with idiomatic use. Some idiomatic chunks are tied to a historical period – *Deep Throat*; some go in and out of fashion – *cool* is 1960s but also twenty-first century, although it was out of fashion in the 80s. Idioms are also related to the genre, age and gender of the user and used for group-bonding.

▶ You will find the activity *Tolerating ambiguity* on page 52, and *Your last chance* on page 96.

The only answer we have for our learners is to raise their awareness. They need time and experience to develop inner criteria and a tolerance of ambiguity, as well as deciding on what they need to know and use in their own idiolect and for what they need only a passive knowledge. The more learners or teachers say *'It depends'* – the better.

## Chunks and language materials

The Lexical Approach, then, is a way of thinking about language which puts lexis before grammar. Lexical phrases or lexical chunks are seen as the crucial building blocks of the language which 'prime' certain grammar – see Nattinger and DeCarico (1992), Lewis (1993) and Hoey (2005). The emergence of this new way of thinking about language coincided with the development of new tools to examine the facts of the language we speak and write. Computer analysis of the language corpus has provided invaluable information about the meaning of words, their frequencies and their word partnerships, and so on.

▶ The activities in Chapters Two and Five go into the issue of language materials more fully.

The analysis of corpus data has revised many long-held beliefs about grammar and lexis and led to a clear distinction between spoken and written grammar. The pedagogical implications for ELT are immense, and the new way of thinking is already finding its way into our coursebooks and other teaching materials, making use of the evidence and insights of corpus linguistics.

### ▪ Chunks and coursebooks

Unfortunately, coursebooks have lagged behind in adapting to the evidence that chunks are important to the learner. Most have it backwards: they teach the grammatical structure and

> For more on the subject, see the section on coursebooks in Part C.

then add the lexis. Approaching the grammar is much more amenable if the lexical chunks are approached *first* – and the grammatical structure is approached *after* the lexis.

It is not an exaggeration to say (at the time of writing) that there are at most only a handful of coursebooks that have any kind of lexical syllabus or that are based firmly on evidence from a corpus in the way they teach lexis. It is worth noting that, although many coursebooks now say on the cover that they have a lexical syllabus and refer to corpus-based evidence, when one looks inside it is clear that this is not the case but merely window dressing.

> See *Vocabulary lists* on page 41.

A simple test of how much a coursebook neglects chunking is to have a look at the vocabulary lists at the end of each unit – they are mostly single words rather than chunks. Getting and collecting chunks around a theme is a useful preparation for speaking tasks and roleplay, and equally good preparation for a written task. Coursebook lexis needs to be extended and contextualised before setting the other tasks.

A simple activity for learners at *any* level is to give out the vocabulary list from the back of a unit of the coursebook. All you ask them to do is add a word or two *before* or *after* the single words which are listed. They can use their knowledge, refer to the coursebook unit, research on the Web or use a good corpus-based dictionary.

### Chunks and grammar books

> You can do *Chunks first, then grammar* on page 50 and *Grammar from chunks* on page 60.

Grammar books, notably the *Cambridge Grammar of English*, are beginning to adapt and give more prominence to corpus evidence and the interaction of lexis and grammar. One day soon, it is logical to assume, there may be a merging of the dictionary and the grammar book – but that may be a long time coming.

Jimmie Hill (in *Teaching Collocation*, 2000) makes the point that progressing from level to level in language learning, especially at higher levels, does not involve just learning new words and new grammar. Most teachers would agree that at higher levels there is hardly any new grammar: most of the structures will have been taught by then.

But what learners *can* do is learn more chunks. In *Grammar and Vocabulary for Cambridge Advanced and Proficiency* (Side and Wellman, Longman 1999) the authors combine grammar and vocabulary/lexical input and practice. But advanced learners can be very consumerist about learning sophisticated vocabulary, and one hundred different verbs describing the ways of walking or looking at something does not automatically make the learner a proficiency-level student. Learning 'old' well-known words in new chunks and contexts – *make headway*, *make of a car*, *make do*, *kiss and make up*, *make the grade*, etc – does. We need to look for materials or design activities which do that consistently and consciously. Learners need to be able to recognise and isolate a chunk (from a text) and then be able to use it correctly in a new context. Our job as teachers is to get them skilled in recognition and application.

### Chunks and dictionaries

> Go to *Be a sport* (page 38), *Bilingual dictionaries online* (page 41) and the activities from page 93 onwards.

There is now a plethora of dictionaries that are corpus-based. This started with the *Collins Cobuild Dictionary* and later the *Macmillan English Dictionary*, and now most modern ELT dictionaries are corpus-based. They are a useful tool if we get our learners to throw out their old dictionaries to buy new ones and then train them to use a corpus-based dictionary which includes the chunks they need along with the definition of a word.

Single words feature as the head entries in dictionaries. However, in any modern corpus-based dictionary there are many examples of chunks (often page after page!) which include the headword and an authentic example taken from the corpus which further clarifies the usage. The frequency of the headword is often given and frequency is also a criterion for whether to include a chunk or not. It is only in the old-fashioned bilingual dictionaries (which some learners still use) that, for example, the word 'take' is translated into a number of verbs without further explanation as to usage, without the relevant chunks and without any authentic examples.

*'Thought is the blossom; language the bud; action the fruit behind it'*
Ralph Waldo Emerson

The first thing is to get our learners (or their parents if they are young) to buy a modern dictionary: then we can get them to look up the word, look for its meaning in the chunk, its place in a chunk, and then learn the whole chunk. When the learners see for themselves that words function in all kinds of chunks, they are more convinced about the usefulness of chunking. The benefit is that chunks speed up the learning process, learners learn 'ready phrases' and use them correctly, aware of differences in form, meaning and usage.

There are also Web-based dictionaries to try out. They can provide a basis for learner training in the use of dictionaries to notice the chunks around a word or around a theme. We have, then, two principles of good lexical training for learners: more use of available information technology (blended learning) and using technology to access data about language (DDL – Data Driven Learning).

Many of the activities in Part B of *The Company Words Keep* exploit Web resources for use in class or for homework and research. Using the various tools available helps learner training, brings IT into class and fosters learner independence. They are also useful for settling quibbles and doubts about the language – for both learner and teacher.

## Chunks and language learners

*'A little is a lot'*
Caleb Gattegno (originator of the Silent Way)

If we can establish awareness of chunks at lower levels, then we can avoid a lot of potential problems later. Asking lower-level learners or younger learners to express themselves in full grammatical sentences is cruel and inhuman – conversations using chunks are a perfect solution to the problem of personalisation, confidence building and freer expression.

### Chunks and beginners

We can have good conversations with our low-level learners of any age when we use chunks. Imagine a conversation with an elementary learner about their last weekend – when the simple past is a structure that has not yet been taught. A recent lesson one of us did started something like this:

► This is also relevant to the points made in *Chunks and children* in Part C.

**Teacher to 11-year-old Maciek:**
- *Maciek. Your weekend … Tell me.*
- *Oh, nice. Very nice.*
- *Your grandmother's house?*
- *Yes, in Malbork.*
- *A long walk?*
- *Yes, to the castle.*
- *And later?*
- *Computer games.*
- *How long?*
- *Two hours. My limit. You know.*

**Maciek then took the initiative:**
- *And you?*
- *Oh typical.*
- *Much work?*
- *Well, some.*
- *And then?*
- *A film on TV.*
- *What title?*
- *Don't remember. About the war.*
- *No walk?*
- *No, too lazy.*

In the exchange above:

- Both speakers, the teacher and the learner, enjoyed equal status.
- The learner made no crucial grammar mistakes.
- Intonation was important to meaning.
- The length and type of chunks varied – from single words, to chunks, to routines.
- The learner took the initiative.
- The learner both made statements and asked questions.

*'Out of intense complexities intense simplicities emerge. Broadly speaking, the short words are the best, and the old words when short are best of all.'*
Winston Churchill

These conversations can be hard for the teacher because you have to stick to chunks and grade your language. But the self-esteem and confidence of the learners and the avoidance of mistakes is paramount. Once the learners have an array of chunks at their disposal, it is reasonably easy to get them to add the grammar later. The *reverse* is not true: and an early emphasis on grammar can lead to lack of confidence and to fossilised grammar mistakes.

> On chunks and lifelong learning, see Part C: 'Chunks and adults'.

### Chunks and advanced learners

Lexical density is a feature of spoken English, and not using all the grammar and lexis you know is an important skill for speaking (rather than 'making a speech'). As David Brazil, in his *Grammar of Speech*, says: *'speech doesn't have sentences'*. So just as we need to encourage lower-level learners to express themselves in chunks, we need to do the same at higher levels. More advanced learners who have not been accustomed to a lexical approach have learnt lots of grammar and lots of vocabulary. But they tend to overuse it, speak 'written grammar' – and end up making a speech. The more chunks they have at their disposal, the more natural-sounding their spoken English will be. And they also need to reconsider and recycle the words they know. Rather than learning more and more obscure vocabulary, they need to learn the environment of the words they *already* know when speaking or writing in English.

### Chunks and ESP/EAP

In a medical English class, it is relatively easy to take a key word, such as 'operation', and build the environment that suits an interest group. So we can get: *emergency operation, routine operation, three-hour operation*, etc. And then we can expand the chunk again: *do an emergency operation, perform a routine operation, undergo an operation*, etc.

> The activities in Part B are highly adaptable to ESP. *Chunks first, then grammar* (page 50) is a good example.

Once the chunks for a certain area are established, it is again relatively easy to add and revise the grammar – by adding time and an adverbial to the chunk: *He underwent a three-hour emergency operation just three days ago.*

The background of the learners is all-important here: working with the word *operation* with military or business people would get a very different result.

### Chunks and exams

Most learners want, eventually, a certificate for their CV. And many answers in most exams are testing learners' knowledge of chunks. Obviously, the multiple-choice and gap-fill, and often the cloze test components of exams are more often than not asking the learners to complete the chunk or display their knowledge of a specific chunk. Let's look at an example:

> See the 'Exercises and exams' section from page 49 onwards.

> *The London Tea Trade Centre is a centre of an industry of … (1) importance in the … (2) lives of the British.*
> 1  A  high        B  wide       C  great       D  large
> 2  A  common   B  typical    C  everyday  D  usual

The way to choose the correct answer is to recognise the two chunks: *of great importance* and *everyday lives*. Learners often argue that *high* or *large* are correct answers in the first example and use their bilingual dictionaries to prove they mean the same as *great*. A good corpus-based dictionary will give the correct answer.

**Error-correction.** Tasks in exams often rely on knowledge of chunks, too. The task set below is to find the mistake by spotting the word which does not belong. In essence, the examiner is 'disrupting' the chunk:

> … *she has been very kindly given me a holiday job. It was difficult in the beginning because I tend to find it very hard to get up in the morning. My boss is very keen on punctuality …*

> Chunks and feedback is examined in Part C on page 106.

In the first line, the addition of the word 'been' is asking the learner to distinguish between two chunks: … *been kind to* … and … *very kindly given* … .

**Register.** In the following task, the learners have to read this original text:

> *Write to all club members to make them feel at home and to give them the latest detail about all the activities coming up soon.*

They then have to fill the gaps in the following text:

> *Dear Club members,*
> *We have an exciting few months ahead of us. The purpose of this letter is to _____ you on our plans for_____.*

They need to know the chunks *update somebody on something* and *plans for the future*. The majority of learners have big problems with this task. Perhaps it is because sometimes they are more familiar with formal chunks and less with informal ones, or vice-versa. In order to succeed in the task, the candidate must be equally familiar with chunks in *both* registers, and be able to retrieve them easily.

**Frequency.** It also seems that examiners are taking account of the interest in lexical chunking to create new exam tasks. The revised CAE and CPE exams have incorporated a new task involving chunks called: 'gapped sentences'. The candidates are given three sentences from which the same word has been removed and they have to find it:

> A. *Melanie practised her lines each day after school, getting increasingly nervous as the date of her audition … even closer.*
>
> B. *Although Tim had been in the lead for most of the race, as they reached the final bend, Graham … level and threatened to overtake him.*
>
> C. *On an impulse, Laura … all the money out of her bank account and went to London, intending to spend every last penny of it.*

▶ See *Gapped with a twist* on page 53 and *Gapped sentences DIY* on page 54.

The word is 'drew' and, in order to find it, the candidates need to know a number of the uses of the verb 'to draw' in different chunks: *the date drew closer, somebody drew level with somebody* and *drew money from the bank*. The way the chunks are chosen seems to follow the principle that there is a chunk the learners learned at *lower levels* (pre-intermediate, intermediate: sentence C), at *higher levels* (upper-intermediate, advanced: sentence A) and at *very advanced level* (proficiency: sentence B).

They are chunks containing the same word, but they are chunks of different frequency. One thing is clear, however, and that is what Jimmie Hill observed: reaching higher and higher levels of proficiency means meeting *old* words in *new* chunks.

**Receptive and productive skills.** In the reading papers in some exams for example, the correct answer is a chunk. In the listening paper, learners may have to listen for a chunk and write it or part of it down on the answer sheet. Productive skills involve a lot of chunking too. Writing tasks and spoken tests are often a test of genre, which in a large part involves knowing the appropriate chunks for the genre. In short, the more lexical chunks learners have at their disposal, the more likely they are to achieve good results.

## Metalanguage

▶ For more on 'language about language', see the 'Glossary of terms' on page 21 and the 'Review' section on page 103.

We know and use metalanguage in our classes and we teach it to our learners. Words such as *definite article*, *perfect tense*, *countable*, *paragraphing* and *secondary stress* are useful for conceptualising, for shortcuts when talking in class and for learners using reference materials for homework or self-study. Metalanguage is also useful when giving feedback to learners, either in class or in their homework.

Talking about and teaching chunks of language requires the use of metalanguage which is specific to this area and approach. So terms like 'deixis', 'colligation', 'word partnerships' or 'lexical density' are needed. Some of these terms are dealt with in depth below and you will find the rest in the Glossary.

As well as supporting a more lexical approach, metalanguage is part of a more humanistic approach to learning. Giving the learners the tools to talk, study or think about the language and their learning needs, or making them figure out grammar rules through the discovery technique, makes them independent and aware learners. The same needs to be done when teaching chunks. Basically, if you believe in using metalanguage for talking about grammar (or pronunciation or writing), then it calls for the use of chunk-related terminology too.

Conversely, if you never use metalanguage in class and believe in covert presentation, you will already have developed your own ways of presenting language without the use of the formal terminology. These same ways will work for getting across the message about chunking.

# Chunks and language learning

It is obviously a presupposition of this book that there should be more emphasis on chunks and, since chunks are more a feature of the spoken, more emphasis on the spoken language too. Learners at all levels, including beginners, need to focus on collecting and expressing themselves in chunks.

So learner training, learner autonomy and awareness-raising are crucial issues. We need to raise *awareness* of chunks at lower levels and change *ways of learning* at higher levels for those who have little experience of 'thinking' in chunks and also need simple activities to raise their awareness.

▶ Chapter One focuses on raising awareness from the first lesson and dedicates several activities to learner training.

## Recognition and retention

Recognising and learning the right chunks is part of learner training and helps to form good learning habits. Learners need to develop the skill of selecting, storing and retrieving chunks: collocational competence. They need to learn from the very start that words appear in certain contexts or environments.

▶ See Chapters One and Two in Part B, in particular.

In a test we were doing with a new class recently, the learners were asked to put 'bear with somebody' into context. The majority used the chunk with the meaning *tolerate*, failing to notice the difference between *bear somebody* and *bear with somebody* (meaning 'be patient') despite some previous work on the problem of chunking. They still have a long way to go! These learners are 'proficiency' level and they *still* need to be taught good habits of language learning and chunks.

▶ The first part of Chapter Three, 'Practice', includes activities to aid retention.

In general, learners need to:

- notice and write in their notebooks (and then learn) full chunks: *take a rest* rather than *rest*;
- notice that words have different meanings in different chunks: *You are tired, I take it. He was taken to court*;
- notice that one form can have different meanings: *take it from me* (meaning 'here it is'), *take it from me* (meaning 'accept what I say');
- notice that small changes in a chunk have a big effect on meaning. *Take a blue and white one* differs from *take a blue one and a white one*.

## Restrictions

Learners also need context to understand the restrictions on the use of a chunk. In a recent class, a learner said '*There is a bone of contention between the two families*'. Good idea – but completely wrong! The restriction is: 'something *is a bone of contention*' or '*the bone of contention is* something'.

## Right and wrong

*'We must escape the tyranny of the correct answer.'*

*'A mistake is a gift to the class.'*
Caleb Gattegno

In essence, we need to get learners to experiment and not think in terms of right and wrong – and to tolerate ambiguity – by getting them to develop their own judgment; to bit by bit develop inner criteria. With word partnerships, some are more *likely* than others – and 'it depends' is often a good answer.

One way to make the learners aware of the phenomenon of chunking is an activity we learned from Michael Rundell. He suggests that, instead of asking the learners to find chunks of language in a text, you ask them to find words which are not part of a chunk. This activity neatly makes the point that more or less every word in any text has a partnership and comprises part of a chunk. In any given text, it is hard to find a word which stands alone.

▶ Again, *Chunks first, then grammar* and *Grammar from chunks* are key activities.

It would seem that lexis is needed *before* approaching grammar, too. We don't think about which tense or other grammar structure we want to use – and then add the lexis. Our first thought is the word; and then we select the chunk, and then the grammar. First, *beer*, then, *nice cold beer*, and only then, *I'm going to have a nice cold beer after the lesson*.

# Chunks and language teaching

*'To simplify complications is the first essential of success.'*
George Earle Buckle

Our conclusion? It is time to pull these threads together – in the teaching of *language*, a more cooperative stance between *learners* and *teacher* is the crucial prerequisite of a more lexical approach.

One of the authors of this book is a native speaker and the other is a non-native speaker. When we are teaching English, we are often faced with a question for which we do not have the answer readily to hand. This is probably for different reasons: the native has the knowledge but cannot access it consciously; the non-native may lack the knowledge or confidence in their knowledge, feeling they are lacking in exposure to real English. It is difficult to give accurate answers off the cuff, so a cooperative stance and recourse to the data will serve our learners.

## ▄ A theory of language

One of us was asked in class which is correct: *'have a bath'* or *'take a bath'*? It is very difficult off the top your head to answer this question with any certainty – we think we know the answer, but it is intuition rather than a fact. When we looked on the Web, we could get data: the British National Corpus had 145 occurrences of *'have a bath'* but only 26 of *'take a bath'*; *Googlefight.com* (a site for comparing frequency of use) has 55,400,000 occurrences of *'have a bath'* but only 23,600,000 of *'take a bath'*. Try 'googlefighting' *have a shower* vs *take a shower* on your computer to see if the result is similar. If you have learners with laptops or a data-projector linked to the Web in your classroom, you can do it in class. If not, you can check it at home or make it an interesting 'mini' homework task.

▶ For more on using data, see Chapter Five and, for specific searches, see *Questions, queries and quibbles* on page 97.

If we accept that chunks are fundamental to learning a language and that a more systematic emphasis on chunks will help our learners, then we need to work out how to *teach* them. Corpus linguistics gives us a fuller description of the language and suggests that we should teach more and more chunks and accustom our learners to noticing, using and collecting them. But this emphasis on chunks – lexis before grammar – is a theory of language. We also need a theory of learning to go with it. Accepting that we need to emphasise chunks more is not enough. How do we do this and what are the implications for our methodology?

## ▄ A theory of learning

Of course, we do already teach a certain number of chunks and so we are just *reemphasising* our practice and taking it a step further. We can do this through learner training, awareness-raising and getting the learners to develop inner criteria and tolerate ambiguity.

- The lexical approach can be seen as conservative, in the sense that it inherently suggests that one's memory is loaded and that language is the retrieval of ready-made chunks from the brain. Almost behaviourist!
- Or it can be seen as progressive, in the sense that it suggests inner criteria and independent learning – developing a feel for what is likely, not what is correct. To feel that 'it depends' is a good answer is a useful skill for learners to have.

*'You only forget what you are asked to remember.'*

*'We talk to express ourselves, if communication takes place it's a miracle.'*
Caleb Gattegno

Our main aim is to get the learners expressing themselves by retrieving the appropriate chunks they have experienced and retained.

We aim to get the learners to develop their perceptions of the patterns; to observe and note. In essence, we propose a bottom-up approach. Rather than a search for the philosopher's stone of a universal grammar that turns base metal into gold, we are looking at what is frequent and useful and in what context it is used. (This in no way conflicts with Chomskian ideas of performance – Chomsky himself, on our reading of his more recent writings, expresses an interest in chunks. He seems to be saying that, although the brain is hard-wired for grammar, we still need to acquire the sounds and the lexis to go with the grammar.) What we aim for, in exposing our learners to the idea and the prevalence of chunks, is to get them 'speaking rather than making a speech'.

*'Though this be madness, there is method in it.'*
William Shakespeare

## A theory of teaching

Since at the moment a more lexical approach seems to be a theory of language waiting for a methodology, a better approach might be to reconcile existing models of teaching with the Lexical Approach. In fact, this has already begun to happen. New editions of coursebooks have an added element which is described in the blurb as 'includes elements of the Lexical Approach'. But this is often just window dressing – just adding the buzz word and a few more exercises on collocations to attract more teachers and learners. Practically no coursebooks have been based on corpus data.

Two models of teaching compliment a more lexical approach. One is the ARC model which was proposed by Jim Scrivener (1994). The other is Task Based Teaching and Learning, as proposed by Sheila Estaire and Javier Zanón (1994) and Jane Willis (1996).

**Jim Scrivener's ARC** model combines *Authentic* use, *Restricted* use and *Clarification*.
- The *Authentic use* aspect suggests corpus analysis, looking at chunks and spoken grammar on the Web. Because this data is authentic, it may not fit with the language in the coursebook or the language that is expected in exams.
- The *Restricted use* aspect suggests learners making their own corpus or making one based on the coursebook, and becoming aware that what is acceptable authentic use of language may not be suitable for tests and evaluated language performance in class.
- *Clarification* suggests giving time to additional activities for consolidation and practice – raising awareness of what is suitable in *authentic* use, and what is *restricted* use of the language.

**Task Based Learning** has lessons or cycles which have stages involving exposure to, analysis of and reflection on the language used. It also proposes ideas for improving the effectiveness of learning (Estaire and Zanón) as well as consciousness-raising activities to identify and process specific language features, bringing up useful words, phrases and patterns to learners' attention, practising words, phrases and patterns from the analysed texts, and entering useful language items in their language notebooks (Willis).

*'Language is time and experience.'*
Caleb Gattegno

We have found that presenting the Lexical Approach within the two models mentioned above makes sense to practising teachers. From our teacher training experience, we can communicate our ideas and classroom experience when we embed the Lexical Approach within this frame.

In sum, the Lexical Approach, Corpus Analysis of the language and Spoken Grammar are here to stay. They are exciting developments in ELT and, personally, we have seen how our teaching and our learners have benefited from them. The Lexical Approach may have to struggle a bit more to find its place in language teaching but, both intuitively and from the evidence, it is a step forward in our knowledge and practice.

▶ If you want to check what you know about chunks and chunking, there is a Glossary of terms on the following pages.

▶ If you are happy to experiment – to try and see what happens – find a few activities in Part B and proceed. You can always refer back to the Glossary at point of need.

▶ If you want to explore and research more – before taking the activities into class – you can proceed to Part C where there is a bibliography and a list of websites. There is also a series of 'mini-essays' that we hope will give further insights for your knowledge and development.

# Glossary of terms

**acronym**
New words made by abbreviating the first letters of the words in a **chunk** (*AIDS*; *laser*).

**active listening**
Showing that you are listening to someone by eye-contact, body language and chunks (*Mmm*; *I know*; *Yeah*); also called 'back-channelling' and 'response tokens'. See also **looking after your listener**.

**alignment**
Organising corpus data visually, with the key word of your choice underlined in all the sample sentences and aligned in one central column. See also **concordance**.

**back-channelling** – see **active listening**.

**binomials**
Fixed expressions which usually take the form of two words, usually linked with 'and' (*nice and hot*; *Mr and Mrs*; *ifs and buts*). Statistically, the most frequent form of **fixed expression**. There are also 'trinomials' (*here, there and everywhere*; *tall, dark and handsome*).

**blended learning**
Learning which combines appropriate use of technology, usually at a distance, with a teacher-led, face-to-face component.

**BNC** – see **British National Corpus**.

**BNC simple search**
A search program attached to the **British National Corpus** that can show the **environment** and **frequency** of a word or chunk.

**brain sludge**
Chunks that are retained by the brain without the person realising it (*Play it again, Sam*; *All you need is love*).

**British National Corpus**
An over-200-million-word collection of samples of modern British English which come from a variety of sources, both spoken and written. Easily accessed and free on the Web. See **corpus**.

**Chomskian competence**
The belief that linguistic knowledge and instinct possessed by native speakers make it possible for them to produce and understand **utterances** in their L1, as well as to decide if an utterance is grammatically correct or incorrect.

**chunk**
A group of words (occasionally one word) which form a socially sanctioned unit of meaning. See also **word partnership** and **fixed expression**.

**cliché**
A **fixed expression** that has lost its original meaning or effect through overuse. Often used **pragmatically** for **language play** or bonding rituals (*break a leg*; *keep right on to the end of the road*) – see also **twisted cliché**.

**collocation**
A likely combination of words that form a chunk; a **word partnership**.

**colligation**
A likely combination of words where there is a grammatical as well as a lexical component (*not surprising*; *afraid to*; *afraid of*).

**concordance**
An extract from a corpus organised with the **key/pivot word** aligned to highlight the environment of a word. ('*Makes the invisible visible.*' – Chris Tribble) See also **alignment**.

**concordancer**
A computer program used for making concordances from a **corpus**. The tool can be accessed free online or can be purchased. See **concordance** and **alignment**.

**corpus**
A body of language stored electronically, which can be sorted to show the **frequency** and the **environment** of a word or chunk, or grammatical patterns.

**Cuisenaire rods**
Rods of different colours and sizes which have been adapted to teach language in a concrete way. See also **Silent Way**.

**Data Driven Learning (DDL)**
Where learners formulate a language question or query, then look at authentic examples such as a **concordance**, notice the real-life context and develop their own insights. See also **deductive** and **inductive approach**.

**deductive approach**
Approaching grammar cognitively by studying the rules and then trying to apply them. An **inductive approach**, in contrast, involves looking at examples of the language in context and trying to notice the patterns and work out the rules before, or instead of, formal study of those rules.

# Glossary of terms

**deixis**
Literally means 'pointing' – words which point backwards, forwards, in or outside the subject of a text. They can indicate, for example, the interpersonal (*I*; *they*; *we*; etc), time (*then*; *now*) and space (*there*; *here*; *that*).

**delexification**
Words such as *take* and *just* used in a chunk without their accepted meaning (*take a bath*; *Can I just ask you something?*).

**delexified verbs** – see **delexification**.

**deterministic grammar**
Grammar that is rigid and so 'determined' (*she goes*, *does she go?*). Contrast with **probabilistic grammar**. ('*A nice place, this*' would be accepted (and even preferred) by most native-speaker communities rather than '*This is a nice place*'.)

**digital immigrants** – see **digital natives**.

**digital natives**
Refers to those who have grown up with the internet and so are 'native' to it. Contrast with **digital immigrants** who have learnt as adults and may be less comfortable with computers and the internet.

**discourse markers**
Words and chunks which soften, lubricate or structure a conversation (*right*; *you know*; *like*; *anyway*; *I see*). Usually aimed at attuning the speaker and the listener to each other or referring to a wider context.

**elision**
When words (or sounds within a word) run into each other. Often involves missing out a sound or sounds and enabling less effort in pronouncing the chunk (*wudya*; *gonna*).

**ellipsis**
Missing out one or more potential words from an utterance, sometimes for effect (*Been there, done that*; *those people … idiots*).

**enallage**
Making a deliberate grammar mistake for effect. Often in songs (*I can't get no satisfaction*) or sporting contexts (*We was robbed*).

**environment**
The normal or most frequent contexts in which a word or chunk occurs. A computer search of a text or **corpus** can organise occurrences of a word or chunk for further study. See also **concordance**.

**ephemera**
Bits of daily life that are usually thrown away, such as tickets, receipts and other pieces of paper. They often contain authentic written-down English chunks that could usefully comprise the text of a lesson.

**filler**
A word or chunk used by the speaker who needs to pause to gather their thoughts but wants to give the **utterance** a smooth feel (*well*; *actually*; *what I was going to say was*).

**fixed expression**
Chunks that are fixed and cannot normally be varied in form or meaning (*by the way*, *Happy Birthday*, *it's not my day today*). Idioms, sayings and **clichés** are normally included in this term.

**frequency list**
A computer analysis of a **corpus** can give the frequency of a word, or compare two or more words or chunks, to find out which is most used.

**genre**
A category or style in writing or speaking with characteristic features of discourse, lexis and grammar.

**hedging**
A cultural tendency in (especially British) English to be less than direct or vague (*I mean*; *sort of*; *kind of*; *rather*; *that kind of thing*).

**holding device**
A word or phrase used in discourse to indicate that the speaker wants to continue an **utterance** (*firstly*; *secondly*; *another thing is*).

**holophrase**
Single words used to convey a complete meaning or thought (*thanks*, *sorry*). Especially used by small children to communicate a wealth of meaning ('juice' can mean '*I want a drink*', '*You are drinking something*', '*It's spilt/finished*', etc).

**idiolect**
The way each person has a slightly idiosyncratic choice of language and chunks which is their own way of expressing themselves.

**incompleteness**
When an **utterance** is unfinished by the speaker but is understood by the listener, thanks to **shared knowledge**. (*Often an utterance is not …*)

**inductive approach** – see **deductive approach**.

# Glossary of terms

**IT immigrants/natives** – see **digital natives**.

**key word**
The word that is highlighted and is of interest when researching chunks using a **corpus**. It is often highlighted in a **concordance**.

**language play**
Using chunks and bits of language differently; playing with language for comic effect or to amuse (*silly me, I'm always doing that – I'd forget my own head*). Children often learn language through playing – rhymes and nonsense words and repetition games.

**lexical density**
The tendency in spoken English to use less grammar but more lexical chunks. Especially true as the conversation progresses and there is more **shared knowledge**.

**lexicographer**
A person who compiles dictionaries nowadays, largely from **corpus** data.

**Linguistic Psychodrama**
A teaching method developed by Bernard Dufeu, making use of the psychological theories of Jacob Moreno to get learners to express themselves through meaningful drama activities.

**link-up** – see **elision**.

**looking after your listener**
Speakers are expected to check that their listener is comfortable and still with them (*You know; yeah? Isn't it?*). Intonation is also quite important here. See also **active listening**.

**metalanguage**
Language used to talk about language, used to help learning (*Can I just ask you something?*). Also the terms which make it possible to talk about language (*deixis*; *ellipsis*).

**mondegreen**
A mishearing of (normally) a song lyric. A term coined by Sylvia Wright who misheard the lyric '*laid him on the green*' as '*Lady Mondegreen*'.

**pragmatics**
The underlying sense expressed by **utterances** rather than their simple surface meaning ('*so then*' expresses a wish to reach agreement and conclude a discussion).

**priming**
By constant use, words and chunks are 'primed' or prepared in the minds of the native-speaker group to have an accepted and specific meaning or to appear in certain grammatical contexts (*drinking problem* is primed to refer to an alcoholic; *a problem drinking* refers to a physical or medical problem).

**pivot word** – see **key word**.

**probabilistic grammar** – see **deterministic grammar**.

**prosody**
The meaning that is conveyed by intonation, stress, tone, etc, rather than by lexis and grammar.

**redundancy**
The fact that not everything is necessary for understanding and that some bits in an **utterance** are like 'background noise' (*Txtspk cd be a gd exmpl*).

**response tokens** – see **active listening**.

**retention**
Ability to store and remember information without conscious effort. ('*Retention is a natural process.*' '*We only forget what we are asked to remember*' – Caleb Gattegno) See also **retrieval**.

**retrieval**
Recalling information and language stored in memory or retained. See also **retention**.

**routine sentence** – see **routines**.

**routines**
Certain fixed utterances which have expected replies ('*How are you?*' '*Fine thanks. And you?*').

**shared knowledge**
As a conversation progresses, we gain more knowledge of the subject and our co-conversationalist(s) and so tend to use less grammar and more **lexical density**.

**Silent Way**
A teaching method developed in the mid-twentieth century by Caleb Gattegno. Main features include the teacher 'doing as little as necessary', learners creating their own text, and the teacher 'forcing awareness' so that the learners develop their own 'inner criteria'; also the use of **Cuisenaire rods** and word charts.

**sketch engine**
A program used by professional **lexicographers** and linguists which is used to sort corpus data about a given word into statistical tables to show its **environment** and the **frequency** with which it co-occurs with other words.

# Glossary of terms

**slot**
A free place or gap in a bigger whole where a word or words can be inserted to complete a phrase or a sentence.

**SMS**
The common international term for what is usually called a text message in British English.

**text message** – see **SMS**.

**textspeak**
One of the many terms used to describe the language **genre** used for text messages. Sometimes called *textspk*, *textese* or **SMS** language.

**tolerance of ambiguity**
The idea that a language learner needs to think in terms of what is likely and unlikely and to develop their own feeling for the language or 'inner criteria', rather than seeking one correct answer. See also **Chomskian competence**.

**twisted cliché**
Making changes to a **fixed expression** for effect – a type of **language play** (*raining cats and dogs* becomes *raining kittens and puppies* for 'light rain'). See also **cliché**.

**trinomials** – see **binomials**.

**Urban Dictionary** – see **wiki**.

**utterance**
The tendency to prefer chunks and **probabilistic grammar** over well-formed **deterministic grammar** when speaking. (*'Speech doesn't have sentences.'* – David Brazil)

**vagueness**
The tendency not to be precise when speaking (*and things*; *sort of*; *whatever*; *kind of*). Often a way of expressing politeness by being indirect, especially by teenagers.

**wiki**
A website created by a group of people who care to participate. Wikipedia is a very well-known example. www.**urbandictionary**.com is an example of a dictionary created for teens by teens.

**word partnership**
A more general term for a **collocation** or a chunk; a likely combination of words.

**word sketch** – see **sketch engine**.

▶ In Part B, you will find that the terms listed above are often used within an activity, either for your own understanding of the rationale behind the purpose of the activity – or, on occasion, for you to be able to explain the concept to your learners: to raise their awareness and direct their learning.

▶ In Part C of *The Company Words Keep*, either working alone or with a colleague, or in the context of a teacher development session, you are invited to check how much you really know about these essential terms – in an interactive way.

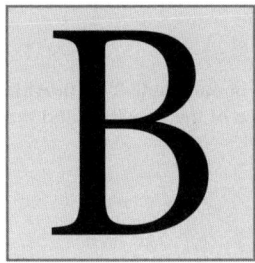

**The Company Words Keep** is at heart a practical book. We pointed out on page 6 how the first concordances of a corpus were based on the Bible in the thirteenth century. Contemporaneously, in 1230, the then Archbishop of Canterbury, Simon Langton, a practical man, invented the idea of dividing a book into chapters. Here are our five chapters of easily usable activities:

## The chapters

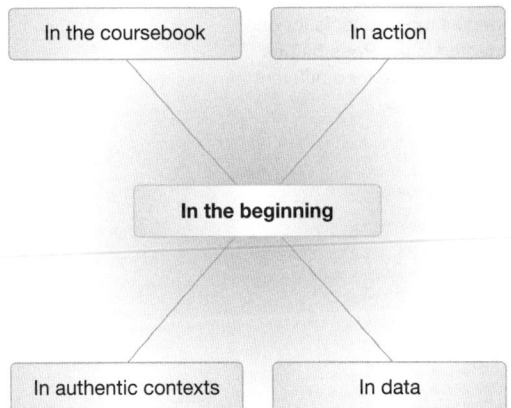

**1 In the beginning**
Introducing learners to the basic ideas of chunking – activities for all levels. Start here before branching out in the direction of your choice.

**2 In the coursebook**
Adding more chunking – to an existing coursebook or exam course.

**3 In action**
Consolidating and practising the idea of chunking – for learners who are already familiar with the idea.

**4 In authentic contexts**
Exploiting chunks in real text – whether written, audio or visual.

**5 In data**
Working with Web resources – to help learners approach chunking directly themselves.

## The activities

**Purpose**
A short description of the intended outcome for the learners.

**Preparation**
What you need to take to class and what resources you might need.

**Procedure**
A step-by-step explanation of how to conduct the activity.

**Possibilities**
How the activity could be varied, extended or adapted for different types of learners.

**Connects to …**
In Part A, we opened *Pathways* to other parts of the book. In Part B, each activity connects to others that you might find suitable, relevant or simply attractive: for you and your learners.

**The level and duration of each activity is provided in graphic form, to give an at-a-glance idea of the activities and their suitability for any classroom situation.**

### Level

■ suitable

▫ adaptable

▫ not suitable

Therefore, for example:

■ ■ ■ suitable for all levels

■ ▫ ▫ suitable for lower levels

■ ▫ ▫ suitable for lower levels
adaptable for intermediate levels
not suitable for higher levels

▫ ▫ ■ not suitable for lower levels
adaptable for intermediate levels
most suitable for higher levels

You will find that an activity which is recommended as most suitable for one particular level has also, very frequently, been adapted in the **Possibilities** – presenting a different focus and using a different procedure for a different level.

### Duration

The estimated duration for an activity is presented as follows:

● ◡ ◡ about 15 minutes

● ● ◡ between 15 and 30 minutes

● ● ◡ about 30 minutes

● ● ● between 30 and 45 minutes

● ● ● about 45 minutes

These suggestions are *estimated*. Before embarking on an activity, and according to the time you have available, we hope you will find it useful to have an idea of its potential duration. But what happens after that – is up to you and your learners.

# Chapter One
## In the beginning

Our first aim is to get learners into the habit of noticing and expressing themselves through chunks: seeing lexis as word partnerships rather than single words. In nearly all the activities, the learners are building and practising chunks from what they already know – recycling or revisiting known words, and expanding them as chunks.

Beginners or elementary learners can be introduced to the idea of thinking in chunks at an early stage, as many of the activities require very little language. There is also an emphasis on speaking.

Higher levels can also do these same activities to get accustomed to the idea of chunks. The core activity can be done quickly – as an awareness-raising activity or a lead-in to a lesson. Often, however, a further possibility is suggested which is definitely more suitable for higher levels and will stretch more advanced learners.

### Learner awareness
The first activities aim to build confidence by demonstrating to the learners that they know more than they think they know.

### Learner training
There are then activities for establishing good practice:
- Organising notes while listening
- Collecting and recording
- Using resources such as dictionaries and the Web
- Getting a first glimpse of what a simple corpus looks like – providing a framework for learners to create their own concordances

These themes are all followed up in later chapters.

## A first lesson

Right from the start, learners are encouraged to use natural lexical chunks rather than unnatural grammatical sentences – they tend to use ellipsis and short forms, anyway, presumably transferring what they would do naturally in their native language.

Level ■ ❏ ❏    Duration ● ● ◐

### Procedure
- In a class of absolute beginners, ask a few students:
    *What's your name?*
- Continue until you are sure the class understand.
- Encourage the learners to give the short answer: *Paul, Hania*, rather than the long answer: *I'm Paul, I'm Hania*.
- Ask a few more learners but, this time, say:
    *And you? And you? You?*
- Get the learners to answer by giving their name.
    - Practise *What's your name?* until they all have reasonable pronunciation.
    - Practise *And you?* and *You?* until they have reasonable intonation.
- Give each learner a blank sheet of paper. Explain (in their L1 if necessary) that, using the questions you have taught them, they have to make a list of everyone's names:
- The learners move around. You join in, too, making your own list.
- Monitor what they are doing. If they are still saying *What's your name?* after the first few times, encourage them to say *And you?* or *You?* more often.
- When they have finished, they write down their list of names and you write up the model sentences *What's your name?* and *And you?* for them to copy into their notebooks.

### Possibilities
■ ■ ■ This activity can be used at *any* level – for group formation and to establish the use of short chunks rather than full grammatical sentences.

■ ■ ■ The learners can compare what happens in English with what the equivalent would be in their mother tongue. Most languages would use short answers and 'ellipsis' (introduce the word using L1 at lower levels). No learners will know the term 'ellipsis' in L1, but the 'idea' is common.

You can make clear that the genre of written English is different from the genre of spoken English.

**Connects to**
*How many words?* (30) ▪ *International words* (31)

## Real classroom routines

This activity forces the learners to become aware of the importance of metalanguage, starting with one of the most basic and common learner utterances. It is also a way of establishing playful feedback, as opposed to potentially judgemental correction.

Level ■ ■ ■   Duration ● ◡ ◡

### Procedure
- The following procedure needs to be done in a light and non-judgemental way to instil, rather than undermine, learner confidence.
- Wait until a learner says: *I have (got) a question.*
- Explain (in the learners' mother tongue if necessary) that although *I have (got) a question* is technically correct, it can sound too direct and that *Can I just ask you something?* is more common and sounds better.
- Write the following on the board:
  *Can I just ask you something?*
- Ask the learner to start again:
  *Can I just ask you something?*
- Do a quick drill if necessary. When their production is acceptable, you reply: *Of course*, and proceed to answer the question and then continue with the lesson.
- Finally, on any subsequent occasion that a learner asks a question in too direct a way, refuse to answer it until you get: *Can I just ask you something?* Reply: *Of course*, answer the question – and then continue.
- Keep up this convention.

### Possibilities
■ ■ ■ This convention can be used as a standard 'correction' technique. When a learner makes an unlikely utterance, like *Don't take seriously what he says*, prompt a different, more likely chunk: *Don't take him seriously* or *Take it with a pinch of salt*.

It is useful to keep a record of these chunks and recycle them later in an activity. For example, jumble up the versions you are insisting on and the original learner versions – and get the learners to sort out which is the most likely one.

**Connects to**
*Conversational manoeuvres* (45) ▪ *Real-life responses* (64)

## Chunks in your head

When speaking fluently, we retrieve whole chunks ready-made, rather than constructing combinations of words. At beginner or even 'pre-beginner' level, learners usually have English language chunks stored in their heads. This activity raises awareness of such chunks – and their different lengths.

Level ■ ■ ■   Duration ● ● ◡

### Preparation
Bring a hundred or more building blocks to class – of different sizes and colours. (Cuisenaire rods are fine if you have them, but any blocks, pieces of card or buttons will do – as long as you have a range of different sizes. The important thing is to have something visual to use in a kinaesthetic way.)

### Procedure
- Have the pile of blocks ready and visible on your desk, and completely clear the rest of the surface.
- Give a few examples of chunks the learners are likely to know, each time putting down a block to represent the chunk – the bigger the chunk, the bigger the block.
- When you have five or six, revise by pointing at the block and asking the learners to repeat the chunk associated with each block. If necessary, explain the meaning.
- Clear the desk. The learners suggest words or chunks, and you represent them with a block of appropriate length.
- When you have six chunks, point to each one and make sure the learners remember which block is associated with which.
- Get another five or six and revise. Then five or six more. Stop at about 20, as the learners won't remember more.
- Finally, go through the blocks, pointing at each one, elicit the associated chunk, write it up and clarify the meaning.
- Discuss the chunks with the whole class. Explain the usefulness of noticing and using chunks rather than single words. Get the learners to notice that chunks can be one or two words – and often up to about seven.

### Possibilities
■ ◡ ◡ You can do the activity in the learners' mother tongue first. It can then be repeated in English.

◡ ■ ■ This is an awareness-raising activity to show learners how they can transfer ideas such as ellipsis from their native language and to get them to realise that a chunk can be one word, two words – or up to seven words.

**Connects to**
*'Brain sludge'* (29) ▪ *Songs in your head* (79)

## Answers to questions

'Incompleteness' is more usual than a full grammatical answer – learners see that chunks come in different lengths and do not always need a lot of grammar to support them. In many coursebooks, grammar is answered with grammar: *How old are you? – I'm 25 years old*. In real life, you don't always hear what you may expect!

Level ☐ ■ ■    Duration ● ● ◡

### Procedure
- Ask the learners to repeatedly ask you the question: *When were you born?* Each time a learner asks the question, give a different answer which is natural and *true for you*. Write your replies on the board:
  *on the 21st, on a Monday, in February, in the morning, in the fifties, last century, I am not telling you …*
- Ask the learners to notice the following:
  - There are many possible different answers.
  - The answers tend to be chunks rather than full grammatical sentences.
- Ask them to work with the question: *Where do you live?*
- Tell them to get a piece of paper and a pen. The learners mingle and ask each other: *Where do you live?*
- Each time a learner answers:
  - It must be a different answer.
  - It must be true.
- Each learner should write down their own answers:
  *Madrid, in Spain, in a flat, on the top floor, near the centre of town, over some shops …*
- After about ten responses, stop the activity and ask a few learners to read out their different answers.
- Pool all the answers by writing them on the board. First, the one-word answers, then two-word answers, and so on.

### Possibilities
■ ■ ■ This activity (learnt from Mario Rinvolucri) can be repeated with a variety of questions. For example: *Who is she? How old are you? Who is your best friend?* It can also be linked to the coursebook syllabus. So when you are doing the future (with the present continuous), you can use: *What are you doing later?*

☐ ■ ■ The learners can shorten or lengthen the chunks written on the board. In this way, for example, *on a Monday* could become *Monday* or *on a very rainy Monday*; *I am not telling you* becomes *not telling you* or *I am not telling*.

**Connects to**
*Rapid repairs* (62) ▪ *What was the question?* (66)

## 'Brain sludge'

This activity elicits known chunks, demonstrating that fixed expressions are often quotations or clichés. It is extremely artificial, but the results are surprisingly natural – playing with language is a natural way of learning – and it leads to work on intonation to bring out the meaning of dialogues.

Level ☐ ■ ■    Duration ● ● ●

### Procedure
- Write on the board a widely-known 'cliché' from literature, a film or a song that everybody is likely to have lurking in their brain. For example: *All you need is love*.
- Ask the learners to shout out similar chunks they know, and write them on the board:

| | |
|---|---|
| To be or not to be | This parrot is no more |
| Frankly, my dear, I don't give a damn | |
| Hasta la vista, baby | All you need is love. |
| It was the best of times, it was the worst of times | |
| Back to black | Once upon a time |

- The more ludicrous the chunks they come up with, the better (it is surprising what the learners know).
- Stop when they begin to dry up, or you have between 12 and 20 examples.
- Make groups of four to six learners. Each group makes up a dialogue containing as many of the clichés from the board as possible:
  - They can use other language to make it coherent.
  - They must use at least six of the ones on the board.
- Give 10–15 minutes to prepare and rehearse, then each group performs their dialogue.

### Possibilities
This is an age-old exercise (learnt from Judy Baker). It is from the *All's Well* coursebook produced more than 30 years ago. Old, favourite coursebooks are sometimes a good source of activities which support a lexical approach.

**Connects to**
*International words* (31) ▪ *Songs in your head* (79)

## How many words?

It isn't always clear when a chunk ends or begins – this activity aims to raise learner awareness by getting them to notice chunks of different lengths while practising extensive listening.

**Level** ■ ■ ■    **Duration** ● ● ○

### Preparation
Choose an extensive reading or listening text suitable for the language level of your learners (a short video extract is ideal). If it is a reading, prepare copies for each learner.

### Procedure
- Ask each learner to take a blank sheet of A4 paper and fold it three times to get eight columns.
- The learners read the text (or listen to the text or watch the video extract) once – or more times if necessary – and note down chunks that interest them, each word in a separate column.
- Pool the results, adding your own contributions and writing them on the board as necessary.
- Discuss.

### Possibilities
The learners often ask for another chance to read or listen to the text after seeing the results of the other learners. Re-reading can be set for homework.

■ ■ ■ In exam exercises, gap-fill and comprehension exercises, the learners obviously need to look at the context to help them get the right answer. If they look at the context in the *adjoining* words *only*, they may miss the part of the chunk that is the vital clue.

**This is an example of the first few chunks from a class listening to *Creature Comforts*, a short humourous animated video:**

| 1 | 2 | 3 | 4 | 5 | 6 | 7 | 8 |
|---|---|---|---|---|---|---|---|
| well | looked | after | | | | | |
| whatever | happens | to | | | | | |
| very | important | | | eat | | | |
| don't | have | much | to | | | | |
| nice | position | | you | comfortable | | | |
| try | to | make | | | | | |
| a | bit | small | | | | | |
| really | happy | | | | | | |
| reasonably | comfortable | | | | | | |
| as | much | as | you | would | like | | |
| go | for | days | without | | | | |
| do | their | own | thing | | | | |
| we | don't | like | ... | we | like | | |
| I | prefer | the | ordinary | kind | | | |
| I | get | ... | and | I | get | ... | and |
| I | don't | like | ... | and | I | don't | like |
| a | big | difference | | | | | |
| sorted | out | | | | | | |
| and | things | like | that | | | | |
| get | out | and | about | | | | |
| stuck | in | all | the | time | | | |
| get | bored | | | | | | |
| same | four | walls | | | | | |

**Connects to**
*Three or five … or more* (32)

## International words

The learners are asked to create simple chunks. This activity introduces the importance of chunks early on, giving the learners a chance to display their general knowledge while making chunks from words they already know, for example the word 'taxi' – *yellow taxis* in New York, *black taxis* in London; and *Taxi Driver*, the movie.

Level ■ ❑ ❑   Duration ● ● ◡

### Preparation
Prepare a list of about 20 international English words that your beginner learners are sure to know. For example: *taxi*, *computer*, *hamburger*. (See below for a fuller list.)

### Procedure
- Write your list on the board (or brainstorm first, to see how many words the learners already know).
- The following English words are usually known by most non-native groups of beginners:

| | | | |
|---|---|---|---|
| taxi | jumbo jet | police | bus |
| satellite | helicopter | cassette | telephone |
| television | computer | video | camera |
| photograph | film | calculator | tennis |
| football | hamburger | sandwich | pizza |
| hot dog | restaurant | supermarket | cinema |

- As an example, get the learners to expand one of the words into a chunk by adding to it before or after, eg *play tennis*, *tennis match*, *tennis player*.
- In pairs or groups, give the learners time to come up with possibilities for the other words.
- Finally, check and pool their suggestions and write them on the board as necessary.

### Possibilities
■ ■ ■ From this lesson on, it is possibly worth making a class rule that the learners are to avoid writing single words in their notebooks, only chunks. This would become part of their 'learner training'.

■ ❑ ❑ It is also possible to get the learners to suggest ways of *reducing* words, so we get *burger* instead of *hamburger*, *phone* instead of *telephone*, etc.

**Connects to**
*Chunks in the picture* (37) ▪ *Vocabulary lists* (41)

## One-word conversations

Although we are more likely to store lexis as multi-word chunks, this activity shows learners that single words are sometimes chunks – especially as a feature of spoken grammar. They, too, are socially sanctioned units of meaning.

Level ■ ■ ■   Duration ● ● ◡

### Procedure
- Get the learners to prepare a dialogue in pairs, to be read out to whole class. Each utterance should have one word and one word only. This is an example of student text:
  - *I…*
  - *No.*
  - *Mm.*
  - *No*
  - *Please.*
  - *Oh.*
  - *Yes?*
  - *Well.*
  - *Thanks.*
- When they are ready, get the learners to read their dialogues out loud.

### Possibilities
This activity looks artificial but, by restricting the learner to single-word utterances, we get a more natural result – which illustrates that lexis is often used at the expense of grammar when speaking. The reading aloud forces learners' awareness of the importance of intonation in conveying meaning.

Instead of presenting the dialogues in front of the class, the learners can circulate their dialogues and read them in pairs. In this way, they get more practice in intonation.

Single-word dialogues often feature in modern literature and can be used in class to get learners used to 'single word chunks'.
This example is from *After Liverpool* by James Saunders:
  - *Hey!*
  - *Hm?*
  - *Catch!*
  - *Thanks.*
  - *Eat!*
  - *Catch.*
  - *Thanks.*
  - *Eat.*
  - *Catch.*

**Connects to**
*Three or five … or more* (32) ▪ *Vocabulary lists* (41)

## Three or five ... or more

Chunks can be more than just a few words. Up to nine is occasionally acceptable if you're repeating the same word. Interestingly, repetition of the *same* word creates *different* chunks. Interestingly, too, even numbers, after two, tend not to be used in spoken English – we repeat three, five, seven or nine times. Repetition is a very common rhetorical device in spoken (and written) English which is often neglected. Here, the learners focus on meaning and intonation – as well as repetition.

**Level** ■ ■ ■   **Duration** ● ◡ ◡

### Procedure

- Write on the board:

  > No
  > No, no
  > No, no, no
  > No, no, no, no, no
  > No, no, no, no, no, no, no
  > No, no, no, no, no, no, no, no, no

- Ask the learners to read the utterances. In what way do they differ?

- Write some one-syllable words on the board. For example:

  > well    wait    right    yeah
  >     stop    mad    sure    please

- In pairs, the learners choose one or two words and experiment with them:
  - How many times can they repeat the word?
  - How does their intonation change?
  - How does the meaning change?

- Ask the learners to move around and deliver their utterances, trying if possible to have a mini-conversation:
  - *Wait! Wait! Wait!*
  - *Yeah, yeah, yeah, yeah, yeah.*
  - *Wait, wait, wait, wait, wait.*
  - *Please. Please. Please.*

- Close the activity by organising mini-presentations of the best exchanges.

### Possibilities

The activity can be repeated with some two-syllable words, for example: *hello*, *thank you*, *okay*.

Some quantifiers work well – *much* and *very* – but only as part of a longer chunk.
So, for example, when teaching comparatives, things are '*much, much, much bigger*' or '*very much bigger*' and '*a bit bigger*'.

You can also make a space in the class or go outside. Stand in the centre of a circle of learners. Walk slowly towards a learner who has to say *Well, well, well* before you reach them. Repeat.
Each learner takes one step backwards.
Repeat a second time, saying *Well, well, well, well, well.*
A third time – one more step backwards:
*Well, well, well, well, well, well, well*
A fourth time – another step:
*Well, well, well, well, well, well, well, well, well*

You can also do the activity as above, but each learner chooses a *different* word.

You can do the activity as above, but if the person in the centre *touches* someone before they manage to say the utterance, they change places.

---

**Connects to**
*One-word conversations* (31)  ▪  *Fixed expression rituals* (65)

## Listening for chunks

When learners listen to authentic text, they can pick up bits of language even if they do not understand every single word. Songs are a good example. This activity aims at making the learners aware of chunks of language when listening.

Level ■ ■ ■     Duration ● ● ○

### Preparation
You will need a recording of a suitable song and one copy of the lyrics per learner.

### Procedure
- Tell the learners they are going to listen to a song.
- Play the song and ask the learners to write down chunks, ie expressions or even whole sentences they hear.
  - They do not need to understand the song as a whole.
  - Their suggestions at this stage can be 'approximate' in terms of accuracy or spelling.
- Discuss with the whole class what chunks they have written down and write them up on the board.
- Play the song a second time.
  - The learners write down any more chunks they think they hear.
  - They notice the ones already up on the board.
- Play the song a third time. Tell the learners to write more chunks.
- Discuss what they have tried to write down, and clarify spelling and meaning.
- Now give out the lyrics. The learners look for their chunks and circle them.
- Discuss with the whole class what 'new' chunks they all think are worth remembering and using.

### Possibilities
This activity encourages the learners to gradually become more aware of their ability to notice chunks, particularly when they are listening to songs. Songs often have 'knocked together' chunks like *omigod* or *woudja* which the learners like to clarify or else they mishear the lyrics as 'mondegreens'.

■ ■ ■ Instead of a song, you can use a video extract of a dialogue, or a short documentary with some commentary. The one-minute news broadcast on the BBC website is ideal.

**Connects to**
*Kiss the sky* (78) • *From English to L1* (81)

## Reading for chunks

This activity involves reading for chunks, and shows how prevalent chunks are. Learners are sometimes asked to notice or collect a few chunks from a text but, here, the point is made that almost everything is connected.

Level □ ■ ■     Duration ● ● ◡

### Preparation
Have a copy of any short text for each learner – either a coursebook text or an authentic one is fine.

### Procedure
- Give out copies of the text and ask the learners to read it, working alone.
- Tell them to find anything which is *not* a chunk.
- Give them a few minutes and then bring the class together.
- Ask for suggestions of what is not a chunk. The learners usually have a few suggestions.
- Throw it open to the class.
- Normally someone else in the class will notice how the word fits into a chunk:
  - On occasion, you might have to point it out.
  - Very, very occasionally, a word stands alone.
- Suggest that since almost all words have partnerships, learners should write only chunks in their notebooks.

### Possibilities
■ ■ ■ You can repeat the activity with a different text but, this time, get the learners to check anything they are not sure is a chunk in a good corpus-based dictionary such as the *Macmillan English Dictionary*. (We learnt this activity from Michael Rundell who was its editor-in-chief.)

■ ■ ■ We have noticed that the vocabulary lists at the end of a unit or coursebook usually focus on and list single words – not chunks. This gives us the opportunity to get the learners to look through their coursebook for chunks and have a 'coursebook corpus' of chunks – a 'lexical chunk approach' to the coursebook.

■ ■ ■ Repeat the activity, but check anything the learners can't chunk against the British National Corpus on their laptops or phones. If you have a connection to the internet, this can be done with the whole class. See Chapter Five for more on using Web resources.

**Connects to**
*Chunks in the news* (74)

## Pass the chunk

This activity demonstrates how a particular word can come in different places within a chunk. With the word *home*, learners are likely to know *at home, home alone, home sweet home*, etc.

Level ▫■■    Duration ●●◡

### Procedure

- Ask the learners to form a circle:
  - The first learner says a chunk – it may come from the coursebook they are using, eg *my mother's cat*.
  - The next learner chooses any word from that chunk and says another chunk that contains the word, eg *my best friend*, or *cats and dogs*, or *my mother's best friend*.
  - The next learner continues – round the circle.
- If you want to make it into a knock-out competition, a learner who cannot think of a chunk, or says a chunk containing a mistake, is 'out'.
- Here is an example of a class response:
  *at home*
  *home alone*
  *home sweet home*
  *short and sweet*
  *sweet sixteen*
  *sweet and sour*
- You can write the chunks on the board for later reference (or correction).

### Possibilities

■ ■ ■ This can also be a writing activity: the learners are given more time to think, they produce a record of their work – and you have a springboard for remedial work.
- The learners sit in a circle of up to ten, each with a blank sheet of paper.
- They write a chunk at the top of their piece of paper and pass the paper to the person on their left, who writes another chunk containing a word from the previous one.
- Continue until everybody gets their original sheet back.
- Display the lists and discuss for correctness.

## Chunking around a word

Chunks can be built up around any key word. 'Colour' is a simple archetype which is of interest to all learners – they can pool and enrich their knowledge of chunks associated with different colours.

Level ■■■    Duration ●●◡

### Preparation

Bring to class one balloon per group of four or five learners. Inflate the balloons (or ask the learners to).

### Procedure

- Divide the class into groups of four or five and give out one balloon per group.
- Tell the learners that they have to keep the balloon in the air by gently patting it.
- As they hit the balloon, they have to say the name of a colour in English; each time a different one.
- Stop the activity as soon as the learners begin to run out of words for colours.
- Tell them to repeat *one* colour and add some words to it.
  - Lower levels might come up with:
    *dark blue, very blue, light blue, navy blue*
  - Higher levels might be able to do more:
    *blue joke, deep blue, black and blue, faded blue, bluey-green, blue moon, blue movie, the blues*
- Again, stop when they are beginning to run out of chunks and change the colour.
- Bring the class together to discuss and write on the board the various chunks they have come up with.

### Possibilities

At lower levels, learners need to know chunks which modify colours (*dark blue, deep blue*, etc).

At higher levels, the learners can exchange their list of chunks, eg *blue sky/blue eyes/feel blue*, etc. Ask them to expand the chunks: *deep blue sky/very blue eyes/feel a little blue*, etc, and add new ones: *blue movie, black and blue*, etc.

You can work with any kind of word sets in this activity, eg animals, parts of the body, etc.

---

**Connects to**
*Chunking around a theme* (36) • *A chunky board game* (44)

**Connects to**
*Be a sport* (38) • *Friendly facilities* (89)

## Nice and easy

According to research, 'binomials' – fixed expressions that cannot be reversed – are the single most common form of fixed expression (idiom) used, so learners should be made aware of them early. *'Nice and …'* would be a simple binomial for lower levels, in conjunction with a lesson on food and drink.

**Level** ■ □ □   **Duration** ● ● ◡

### Procedure

- Brainstorm and write on the board the names of a few of the learners' favourite food and drinks. For example:
  *coffee   beer   pizza   pasta   salad   coke*

- Write the following frame on the board:
  *nice and …*

- Give or elicit an example: 'coffee' could be *nice and hot* or *nice and strong*.

- Ask the learners in small groups to make suggestions for the other words written on the board.

- Check their suggestions and write them on the board:
  beer – *nice and cold*
  pizza – *nice and tasty*

- Finally rub off the binomials and set up the following frame for mini-dialogues in pairs:
  - *How's your …?*
  - *Mmm … nice and …*

- The learners practise with the food and drink words they originally brainstormed onto the board:
  - *How's your coffee?*
  - *Mmm … nice and strong.*

### Possibilities

■ ■ ■ Since binomials are so frequent, it is worth revising and recycling them. You can collect them from authentic texts, from the coursebooks the learners have used – or from examples *they* come across outside the class.

You can present other forms of binomials, other than those joined by *and* – such as *or* and *but*.

As a quick revision exercise, you can prepare, or get the learners to prepare, different words on two slips of paper and do a simple matching exercise:
boys and …   girls       Mr and …     Mrs
ladies and … gentlemen   Lord and …   Lady

The learners are given a beginning or an end, and have to move around to find their partner.

□ ■ ■ The learners can be given the task of contextualising irreversible binomials by creating mini-dialogues of their own:
- What did you do at the weekend?
- This and that.

- Did you do it all?
- By and large.

- Did you sleep OK?
- No, I was tossing and turning all night.

This can be followed by a 'milling and matching' activity. The learners copy each line of the exchange on a separate piece of paper. You mix them up, each learner chooses one – and has to find their partner.

In Wikipedia, search for 'Siamese twins (linguistics)' to get lists. You can cut and paste, and then photocopy them or bookmark them for class use if you have a Web connection available.

### Trinomials

■ ■ ■ The learners may be less familiar with trinomials – see the examples below. Again, there are also a lot of resources in Wikipedia.

---

**Binomials with 'and'**
bed and breakfast
hide and seek
law and order
out and about
toss and turn
bread and butter
high and mighty
neat and tidy
nice and cool
bacon and eggs
spick and span
cash and carry
hit and miss

odds and ends
mix and match
by and large
dos and don'ts

**With 'or'**
now or never
for or against
one or the other

**With 'but'**
oldies but goodies
simple but effective
naughty but nice

---

**Trinomials**
*wine, women and song*
*cool, calm and collected*
*morning, noon and night*
*this, that and the other*
*here, there and everywhere*
*sex, drugs and rock 'n roll*
*ready, steady, go*

---

**Connects to**
*Old words, new partnerships* (73)

# Chunking around a theme

*'Eight minutes past four'* is fine if precision is needed (eg for train times). But coursebooks often fail to teach 'vagueness' when talking about the time. *'Just gone ten past four'* is common in spoken English. Most other languages have such chunks, and learners simply need to transfer the concept from L1.

Level  Duration

## Preparation
Bring to class the sample text below.

## Procedure
- Write the following text on the board.

|   |   |   |   |   |
|---|---|---|---|---|
|   | past | to | a | at |
| one | two | three | four | five |
| six | seven | eight | nine | ten |
| eleven | twelve | quarter |   | twenty |
|   | twenty-five | half |   |   |
| almost | nearly | just gone |   | about |

- Ask for 'time' chunks using only the words you have on the board.
- Give the learners a minute or two to think.
- Brainstorm suggestions and write them on the board. For example:
  *half past two*
  *ten past two*
  *twenty-five to ten*
  *just gone five past six*
  *almost ten*
  *about a quarter to five*
- If the learners have enough language, ask them to personalise the text. For example:
  *I get up at half past seven.*
  *We finish at a quarter to five.*
- If the learners are low-level, elicit a few chunks as short answers to questions like these:
  *What time did you get up?*
  *When do we finish?*
- Finally, ask them to translate *about*, *almost* and *just gone* into their mother tongue. When would they use these vague expressions rather than a precise time?

## Possibilities
You can test the learners by writing up a few times on the board as numbers, eg 4.08. The learners verbalise: *'Almost ten past four'*. After they get the idea, hand it over – for them to test each other.

Write the following text on the board:
*a    this    the    coming    after*
*before    later    ago    next    last*
*yesterday    today    tomorrow*
*day    week    fortnight    month    year*

Ask the learners to come up with chunks for time, using only the words on the board. For example:
*a week today*
*the day before yesterday*
*this time next week*

Write up the following structures:
*I was …*
*I've been …*
*I'll've …*
*I'll be …*
*I …*

Ask the learners to personalise the chunks on the board with true statements. For example:
*I was off school the day before yesterday.*
*I'll be taking my driving test a week today.*

This activity can work around other themes besides 'time': shopping, classroom language, travel, etc.

**Connects to**
*Be a sport* (38) • *Chunks first, then grammar* (50)

## Chunks in the picture

This activity helps the learners to experiment with chunks and notice word order in chunks by describing a picture. It can be used as a preparation for speaking or writing activities. The learners are creating their own 'wiki-corpus'.

Level ■ □ □    Duration ● ● ◡

### Preparation
Prepare a set of different pictures or photos, one per pair of learners, and approximately ten slips of paper per learner.

### Procedure
- Spread out the pictures or photos on tables. One per pair. Give each learner a set of ten blank slips.
    - They work in pairs, mingle and look for English words for things that appear in the pictures. For example: *red, woman, big*.
    - They write the words on separate slips of paper and leave them next to the picture, face up.
    - They then move on to another picture.
- Make sure they write single words at this stage, not phrases or sentences.
- Stop when the learners have used up most of their slips.
- In pairs, the learners go from picture to picture and identify any words written on the slips that they don't know. They can ask the teacher or their classmates.
- Stop the activity when you see they have seen most of the pictures and worked with most of the words on the slips.
- Now ask the pairs to take pens and move from picture to picture. This time, they add one word to the words on the slips – *red hair, young woman, big car*. They write their words on the slips. Make sure the word order is correct.
- Stop the activity when most of the words have been made into two-word chunks.
- Tell the learners to keep moving around. This time, they add a third word where it is possible. You will need to monitor and check, eg *big red car* rather than *red big car*.
- Discuss the various chunks with the whole class.
- Display the pictures, along with the chunks, on the wall or other display area for further reference. The learners are usually interested to see what the others have written.

### Possibilities
This can be followed up by a writing or speaking activity in which the learners describe the pictures, using the chunks.

**Connects to**
*Skilful monologue* (61) ▪ *Picture this!* (93)

## Get this!

This activity trains the learners to revise lexis while learning to scan for 'delexified' verbs (ones that lose their original meaning in the context of a chunk). They also create a simple corpus from the coursebook.

Level □ ■ ■    Duration ● ● ◡

### Preparation
Have sheets of blank A4 paper and the coursebook ready. Before class, choose a number of delexified verbs that you would like to revise. For example: *make, get, take, do, come, set, have*.

### Procedure
- Divide the class into groups. Allocate one delexified verb per group. Tell the groups to keep the verbs a secret.
- Ask the learners to have a look through the last few units they have done in their coursebook. They have to find five to eight examples of chunks with the verb they have been given.
- Give each group an A4 sheet, folded down the middle.
    - On the left, they write down all the examples they find: *get tired, get angry, get out*, etc.
    - On the right, they write a translation in L1.
- Give them time to do the task.
- Now circulate the folded sheets from group to group, with only the translated half visible. The learners read the translations and try to think of the verb. They can then check by looking at the English examples.
- Discuss with the learners what they think they have done. If necessary, point out that they have learnt to scan and note-take.
- You might like to compare the grammar of the learners' L1 with English. Is delexification more a feature of English?

### Possibilities
■ ■ ■ The learners are, in essence, creating a mini corpus and so it is a good preparation if you want to introduce them to the idea of a corpus.

You can, instead of delexified verbs, choose other grammar categories, such as prepositions or nouns.

**Connects to**
*Gaps with a twist* (53) ▪ *Grammar in chunks* (63)

# Be a sport

Modern corpus-based dictionaries may be relatively unfamiliar to learners. This activity shows how modern dictionaries are likely to give the partnerships and context the learners need to understand and use the word in a meaningful chunk.

**Level** ▫ ▪ ▪      **Duration** ● ● ●

## Preparation
You need a set of various dictionaries, some old-fashioned and some corpus-based.

## Procedure
- Choose a very simple English word, ideally one that is a cognate in the learners' L1. For example: *sport*. Write the word in the middle of the board.
- Ask the learners to work in threes and to come up with as many meanings and chunks with the word that they can think of.
- Pool the findings and write them on the board. As far as possible, similar ones should be grouped together.
- Give out the dictionaries and ask the learners to research the word
- Add their new findings to those already written up.
- Discuss with the learners what they have discovered about the word *sport*, and how a word only becomes meaningful in a chunk.
- Assuming the class is using a variety of different types of dictionary, ask them which ones deal with word partnerships and chunks best.

## Possibilities
▫ ▪ ▪ If you divide the class into groups to research a different word, the groups then exchange their findings, which can also be prepared as posters and displayed.

In this activity, the learners are creating their own mini-corpus showing the environment of a chosen word ('sport' in the sample text).

It is also a good opportunity to check their knowledge of a few words of metalanguage: *corpus, corpus-based dictionary, environment, word partnership, concordance, alignment* – in preparation for later activities dealing with corpus and concordances.

---

This shows the end product when learners have pooled what they *know* and added what they have *found* in the dictionaries.

*to make sport of*
 = joke about

*It's sporting of you*
 = generous

*It's a sport*
 = gamble

*to sport shoulder-length hair*

*Hello, sport!*
 = mate

*sportsmanship*

*He is a good sport*

*SUV*

*spoilsport*

**sport**

*sport supplement*

*sports car*

*sportive*

*a sporting chance*
 = likely

*sporting occasion*
*sporting family*      *sports drink*
*sporting hero*

*sportscast*
*sportscasters*

*sports jacket*   *sporty*
         *Sporty Spice*       *sports centre*

---

**Connects to**
*Chunking around a theme* (36) ▪ *Chunking around a word* (34)

## Urban dictionary online

The learners read for specific information and research using print dictionaries and online dictionaries. This activity is also a clarification of the idea of register, since they are being asked to compare a wiki-dictionary compiled by teens with a conventional dictionary.

Level ❏ ■ ■   Duration ● ● ◡

20 minutes, then homework, then 20 minutes

### Preparation
You need representations of different colours (for example cut-up coloured card or different coloured buttons). You will need several of each primary colour. The class need to have access to the internet and/or a good dictionary at home.

### Lesson One
- Lay out the coloured cards – each learner chooses an example of their favourite colour.
- Put the learners into a group with people who have chosen the same colour. If some groups are large, split them into pairs or threes.
- Give the groups a few minutes to chat about their choice of colour: why chosen, associations, etc.
  - Ask them to explain what their colour means in their *first* language and what the connotations are. Give them a minute or two for this.
  - Ask them to speculate what the colour means in *English* and come up with any fixed expressions they know which use the colour.
- Set the homework – the learners have to research the primary meaning of their colour, and bring two or three chunks containing their colour to class.
- Ask each of the pairs/threes which of them is going to research online and who is going to use a dictionary.
  - The onliners are recommended the following website: *www.urbandictionary.com*. (In our experience, many teenage learners will know this website already.)
  - The dictionary researchers will need to use a good corpus-based dictionary to get good results.
- Tell them when you want the data for and that the homework will only take about 15 minutes to do. They must remember who their partners are.

### Lesson Two
- The learners find their original partners and pool and compare their results. (If some haven't done the homework, put them in a group with dictionaries or laptops – to do it now!)
- Put the learners into larger groups, to compare the results for different colours and/or do a short plenary session to compare results.
- Finally, ask them to comment on the different 'takes' on the word by print dictionary and wiki-dictionary compiled by teens.

### Possibilities
Older teenagers will often have come across the urban dictionary site when researching the lyrics to their favourite songs or whatever. They are probably already aware that what they know from the media and what they learn in their lessons are two different things. But it is worth bringing this out into the open in class.

The urban dictionary is rather obscene, with lots of sexual and drug references – you have to be prepared for this and may like to *avoid* this activity with younger or immature classes (although no doubt they access the website in their own time, so we are probably not really protecting them!).

**Connects to**
*Chunking around a word* (34)

# Translate that!

This activity encourages the learners to use their L1 as a resource, by comparing the grammar of English with their own language and noticing the differences. It also expands their knowledge of fixed expressions and introduces the idea of deixis ('pointing' words).

**Level** ◻ ■ ■    **Duration** ● ● ◡

## Preparation
Have a copy of a text ready (see the sample opposite) to dictate to the learners.

## Procedure
- Ask the learners for the direct equivalent of the word 'that' in *their* language.
- Dictate the chunks opposite, one by one, and ask the learners to translate them into their first language and write them down. The translations should be as natural and idiomatic as possible. (If it is clear they don't understand one of the examples, give them a context to help with the meaning.)
- When you have dictated all the chunks, ask the learners to get into threes to compare their translations.
- Finally, get them to say how often the direct equivalent of *that* in their mother tongue is the best translation.

## Possibilities
Referring the learners to their knowledge of L1 through translation is an efficient tool for getting them to notice the use of 'that' in English. The word is probably near two percent of spoken English and two percent of written English – and needs supplementary and review activities.

The activity is a variation on one by Mario Rinvolucri and Paul Davis in *More Grammar Games*, CUP. Delexified verbs and the use of deixis (*that*, *it*, *this* – 'pointing words') are a feature of English. If they compare English to L1, the learners come to terms with how different this may be.

◻ ■ ■ This activity works as well with multilingual classes as it does with monolingual ones. Group the learners according to their L1. (You may need a 'miscellaneous' group of people in the class who do not have someone with the same L1.)

---

1 *Thank you for that.*
2 *This and that.*
3 *How about that.*
4 *It's not that ...*
5 *It's that simple.*
6 *It's as simple as that.*
7 *Have you got that ashtray?*
8 *That's just it.*
9 *That's the thing.*
10 *That's the stuff.*
11 *Not that again.*
12 *It's just that ...*
13 *There's something in that.*
14 *That's the question.*
15 *That's that.*
16 *That's it, then.*

**Connects to**
*L1–L2 translation* (48)

# Bilingual dictionaries online

The learners use online translation dictionaries more effectively, noticing chunks – not just the headwords.

Level ■ ■ ■     Duration ● ● ○

## Preparation
Research suitable dictionaries (English–L1/L1–English) online. Choose one (eg http://www.ling.pl/ for Polish learners) which translates chunks rather than word for word. Prepare a list of single words in the learners' L1 for which you think they will know the English equivalents. Write each word at the top of a separate A4 sheet, a different word for each group of learners. You need internet access for each pair or group. (Alternatively, adapt the activity for homework.)

## Procedure
- Divide the learners into small groups around a computer and give out the A4 sheets you have prepared.
  - They look up the English translation of the word.
  - They then look at the chunks given by the website that include the key word.

> Key word: *dom* (Polish) Translation: *house/home*
> ■ house
> the White House – *Biały Dom* / house owner – *właściciel domu* / to run the house – *prowadzić dom* / house-to-house sale – *akwizycja*
> ■ home
> holiday home – *dacza* / to go home – *iść do domu* / there's no place like home – *Nie ma jak w domu* / old people's home – *dom starców*

- Ask the groups to select six chunks, and include the key word.
  - They copy the chunks onto a piece of paper and pass their sheets on to another group.
  - The group give their own translations of the chunks in their L1.
- When the learners have worked on a few of the lists, display them on the wall and give them time to read all the lists and discuss the results. How often is a chunk translated with a chunk? How often with a single word?

## Possibilities
■ ■ ■ When the groups pass on their sheets for the first time, they can look at the list of chunks then write a *new* chunk in English containing the *original* key word. The next group has to research and find an equivalent in their L1 – this way, the list of chunk groups keeps expanding.

**Connects to**
*Dictionary versus dictionary* (93)

# Vocabulary lists

Coursebooks usually have a word list at the end of each unit – often lists of *single words* which are not exploited enough. Learners need to use these words in chunks and begin to *think* in chunks and *learn* in chunks.

Level ■ ■ ■     Duration ● ● ◡

## Preparation
Select a vocabulary list from the end of the unit in the coursebook you have just finished. Make copies if you think the students won't want to write in their books. (Good corpus-based monolingual dictionaries would be useful.)

## Procedure
- Direct the learners to the vocabulary list you have selected, or give out your handout.
- In pairs, they have to take the single words and come up with up to five different chunks, using each word. Encourage chunks of varying length, including whole routine sentences for each word.
- The learners write down the chunks they have come up with. You monitor and check – they can also look for more chunks in the main body of the coursebook.
- Give out the dictionaries: the learners can take a quick browse to get some inspiration from the examples there.
- Regroup the learners – two pairs making a group of four. They pool their chunks.
- With the whole class, discuss in what situations and with what intonation the chunks could be used.

## Possibilities
■ ■ ■ You can do this activity *before* you do the unit in the coursebook. When it is done *after* it is a good review but, done *before*, it is a good preparation for listening and reading activities, and will also help the learners perform better in speaking and writing – since they will have the chunks 'ready and waiting'.

The learners can work in pairs on a different set of words from the vocabulary list. Then they present their ideas to other pairs, who suggest more chunks if possible.

The coursebook series *Outcomes* (Heinle) has a good idea for a 'vocabulary builder': When a new word appears – or an 'old' word in a new chunk – record it, and a few chunks in which it appears. For example:
Elementary – **busy**: Sorry, I'm ~ / have a ~ life / a ~ day …
Advanced – **register**: ~ as unemployed / the electoral ~ …

**Connects to**
*Gapped sentences DIY* (54) ▪ *International words* (31)

## A class concordance

In this activity, the learners revise and pool the chunks already in their heads to make a class concordance with alignment. It shows them how much they know, so building up their confidence.

Level ■ □ □   Duration ● ● ◡

### Preparation
Choose a few frequent words that you would like to revise.

### Procedure
- Write one of the words you have chosen to revise on the board. It should be at the top, in the middle:

    *at*

- Give the learners a couple of examples of chunks with 'at', ask for a couple more suggestions and write them on the board:

    | at home | look at |
    | at five o'clock | looking at me |

- Pair the learners and ask them to come up with more chunks with 'at'.
- Make bigger groups and get them to compare their chunks.
- Finally, ask them to produce a class concordance, writing their chunks in alignment on the board.

    |  | at home |
    | look | at |
    |  | at five o'clock |
    | looking | at me |

- Repeat with another word, perhaps a noun or a verb for a change.

### Possibilities
■ ■ ■ The learners can produce a concordance in poster form and display it in class. Different groups can work on different words.

■ ■ ■ At the beginning of the activity, you can ask the learners how many chunks they know with the key word – they tend to underestimate. At the end, ask them to compare their estimate with the number they came up with. This will normally show they know more than they *think* they know.

**Connects to**
*Learner concordances* (42)

## Learner concordances

This activity introduces or revises the idea of concordances and the alignment of key words, and raises awareness of the importance of chunks to give shades of meaning to a word. The learners become aware a key word may be at the beginning, the middle or the end of the chunk.

Level ■ □ □   Duration ● ● ◡

### Preparation
If the learners have never seen a concordance or alignment, copy a sample or bookmark one on the Web to show them.

### Procedure
- Show or remind the learners what a concordance looks like. Give them a high-frequency word – like 'thing'.
- Ask the learners to remember, or look through their books, and note down as many expressions as possible which include the word. They only need to write full sentences when a sentence is necessary to give the meaning. Different learners can consult different chapters.
- Pool the findings on the board – then make a concordance, with the key word going down the middle:

    > give me that thing
    > What a thing to say!
    > one thing led to another
    > The thing is that …
    > the right thing to do
    > How are things?
    > a thing of the past

- Discuss how useful it is to have the *before* and *after* – the 'environment' of a word. Establish that the frequency and the *environment* of a word are essential to meaningful use.

### Possibilities
□ ■ ■ A useful follow-up to this activity is to check the chunks with a good corpus-based dictionary to show how to use dictionaries to get the appropriate chunks for subsequent speaking or writing activities.

You can choose a word or words which occur in more than one grammar category, getting the learners to show the environment of the word when it is an *adjective*, a *noun* and a *verb*.

If you have the possibility, you might show the learners the raw data of the key word in the British National Corpus. (See Chapter Five.)

**Connects to**
*Going for a song* (91)

# Chapter Two
## In the coursebook

Many coursebooks neglect lexis. They often lack a systematic lexical syllabus (in spite of what they proclaim) and are not based on corpus data.

They often present the grammar structure first and lexis second:
- If learners have the chunks prepared *before* a grammar presentation, the presentation is likely to be easier and more successful.
- If they have the chunks prepared, they are likely to be more fluent and accurate in speaking and writing tasks in class – which is good for exam training too.

The activities here ask the learners to go deeper into meaning by doing the coursebook activities more creatively. They stretch the learners, asking them to 'do a bit more'.

## Games
The first activities are games which can substitute dry exercises. They aim to revise the coursebook lexis but they can also be used with activities from Chapter One to introduce the idea of chunking. All three are for lower levels but can be adapted as awareness-raising at higher levels.

## Dialogues and texts
Coursebook content can be formulaic, repetitive and unnatural for learners (and teachers!). Our activities aim to enliven the presentation or revision of dialogues and texts, while getting the learners to be more adventurous. The activities for lower levels stretch the learners and so can easily be adapted for higher levels.

## Exercises and exams
Coursebooks are full of exercises which are seen as necessary consolidation and are often designed to accustom learners to an exam format. Here, we look not only at the exercise *content* but at the process of how they *work* and how the instructions can be *interpreted*, asking the learners to be creative and make their own exam questions. By getting inside the mind of the examiner, the learners can become more confident in tackling exams. Many of the activities are at quite a high level, although some can be adapted for lower levels.

## Draw a chunk

The learners revise and pool chunks centred around a topic area or a subject from a unit in their coursebook. This fun activity employs a visual element, which is very important for some learners.

Level ▪ ■ ▪    Duration ● ● ◡

### Preparation
Prepare a list of the chunks you want to revise and write them on individual slips of paper.

### Procedure
- Choose one chunk to illustrate the activity. For example: *run a successful business*
- Draw on the board one element of the chunk, eg '*run*'.
- When they have guessed *run*, ask the learners to pool the chunks that come to their minds with the word *run*.
- Draw *business* and *success(ful)*.
- Keep drawing until the class guess the chunk.
- A learner can now take your place.
- Give the learner a new chunk to draw, and the whole class do the guessing.

### Possibilities
▪ ■ ■ You can ask the learners to look through the coursebook units you want to revise and note down five to eight chunks relating to a subject:
- The learners get into pairs or groups.
- One learner draws the whole chunk.
- The others guess what the chunk is.
- They take it in turns – drawing and guessing.

The activity can also be carried out as a competition.

**Connects to**
*Picture this!* (93) ▪ *Picture dictionaries online* (94)

## A chunky board game

The learners retrieve chunks from memory and work on accuracy in the production of chunks. The activity encourages them to experiment, extending single words – and expanding them into meaningful chunks.

Level     Duration ● ● ○

### Preparation
Prepare a grid for a simple board game and write key words in each box (see the example below). Make enough copies for groups of three or four learners, and bring enough dice to class.

### Procedure
▪ Tell the learners they are going to play a board game to practise some of the vocabulary from the coursebook. Everyone needs their own counter (eg a coin or a ring).

| START → | ON | SEE | SURE |
|---|---|---|---|
| IN | GET | NO ← | PERSON ↓ |
| MAKE → | WHITE | SMILE | NEW |
| FINISH | WORK | FINE ← | PAY |

▪ Divide the class into groups of three or four learners, distribute the boards and dice, and explain the game:
  - They throw the dice.
  - As they move onto a square, they must say a chunk with this word.
  - The rest of their group decide if they think the chunk is correct.
  - If it is not correct, the learner has to go back three spaces.
  - If a group cannot decide whether a chunk is OK, they can call you in to check.
▪ The winner is the person who finishes first.

### Possibilities
▫ ▪ ▪ The learners can be asked to come up with five chunks rather than one; or chunks with three or more words.

▪ ▪ ▪ You can give blank boards to the groups and the learners write the key words for the chunks themselves. When they have made their boards, they exchange them with another group, or the games can be used during another lesson.

**Connects to**
*Chunk Bingo (85)*

## Mime a chunk

The learners are asked to memorise and recycle chunks as a preparation for fluency. Some learners will remember chunks better because of the kinaesthetic, fun aspect of this activity.

Level     Duration ● ○ ◐

### Preparation
Have a recording from the coursebook ready – one that you have previously done in class. On separate slips of paper, write chunks from the script, one slip per learner. If the class is very big, prepare sets for smaller groups.

### Procedure
▪ Play a recording the learners have heard before – as a reminder. Tell them to listen carefully because there will be a mini-test.
▪ Give out the slips of paper with the chunks written on them, telling the learners to keep them secret.
▪ The learners stand and make pairs:
  - One learner mimes their chunk.
  - Their partner has to identify and say it.
  - They exchange roles.
  - They exchange slips.
▪ The learners move around, forming new pairs and miming their new slips with their new partner. Again, they exchange slips before moving on.
▪ Stop the activity when it becomes hard for the learners to find a partner they have not yet worked with.
▪ Finally, they get into the order in which their slips appear in the text.
▪ Play the recording once again, if the learners need to check.

### Possibilities
▪ ▪ ▪ The learners can select the chunks from the tapescript themselves and prepare them on slips of paper. You mix the slips and redistribute them. It doesn't matter if some of the chunks are repeated.

You can recycle a song or a reading text in the same way.

**Connects to**
*Draw a chunk (43)*

## Recycling a dialogue

In this activity, the learners get a lot of practice with chunks, through selection, creative use and comparison of texts.

Level ■ ■ ■     Duration ● ● ◡

### Preparation
Select a coursebook dialogue that the learners have already done. (You may wish to prepare a handout of the dialogue for them to write on.)

### Procedure
- Give the learners a minute or two to re-read and remind themselves of the dialogue.
- They work in pairs and underline between about 10–12 fixed chunks or 'routines' that they like or think are useful for speaking.
- Ask them to write a dialogue of about six to eight lines, using only the items they have selected:
  - They must not change or add anything.
  - They can use them in any order.
  - They don't have to use all the ones they have selected.
  - They can refer back and select others that fit.
- This is a text from our learners, based on a much longer dialogue of some 15 exchanges:

> Look! Hurray.
> And the winners are …!
> That's incredible!
> Lucky you.
> That's absolutely brilliant!
> I am happy.
> Me too.

- When the learners are ready, they circulate the dialogues or, in pairs, act out their own dialogues in front of the class.

### Possibilities
■ ■ ■ You can allow the learners to make changes in the chunks or utterances when they write their dialogues. This obviously makes it rather easier – but less interesting, and with less intonation practice.

**Connects to**
*Chunks in novels* (76) ▪ *Shadow thinking* (47)

## Conversational manoeuvres

The learners are made to realise that the same chunk can be used in more than one context and can have a variety of meanings, depending on context and intonation.

Level ◻ ■ ■     Duration ● ○ ◡

### Preparation
Choose a few coursebook dialogues. (You may wish to prepare a handout with the dialogues you have selected.)

### Procedure
- Write on the board a chunk you have taken from a coursebook dialogue you have recently worked on. For example: *Excuse me!*
- Ask the learners to recall what the situation in the book was – in this case, apologising for not doing something.
- Ask the learners to come up with various situations in which they could use the chunk. Write their suggestions on the board. These are examples from our learners:

> *You bumped into somebody. | You are attracting somebody's attention. | You are interrupting somebody. You are irritated with what somebody is saying. You broke a vase. | You don't understand. You don't hear. | You are denying an accusation.*

- In pairs, the learners practise saying the chunk with appropriate intonation – according to the situation.
- They then say the chunk in front of the whole class. The others have to guess the context.

### Possibilities
■ ■ ◻ The learners can use their first language as a resource, translating the fixed expression into L1 and brainstorming the situations in which it can occur. They then use the different intonations that would occur in L1. Finally, repeat the process in English – you translate the situations and help with intonation.

◻ ■ ■ The learners collect a number of expressions from the coursebook, copy them onto slips of paper and put them in a hat or a box. One learner draws a slip and reads it out, focusing on the intonation. The others suggest a different intonation. When they have finished, they draw another slip.

Single words are units of meaning and often act as chunks. Words like *sorry*, *well* and *cheers* work well with this activity since they have a variety of meanings in spoken English, depending on the context and intonation.

**Connects to**
*Real-life responses* (64) ▪ *Questions, queries and quibbles* (97)

## Reduction

This activity raises awareness of the importance of lexical chunks rather than full grammatical sentences in spoken English. It shows how key chunks can convey the intention of the speaker and demonstrates the importance of intonation.

Level ■ ■ ■    Duration ● ○ ☽

### Preparation
Select a text which aims to practise spoken English from the coursebook; or a new text or one you want to review. Often, coursebook dialogues which claim to be 'spoken English' are too formal and more characteristic of written grammar – choose one of those. Prepare one copy per pair of learners.

### Procedure
- Show the learners the dialogue you have selected, and copy the first line onto the board. For example:
  *So what are your plans for today?*
- Ask the learners to cross out the words that can be removed. Emphasise that the message has to remain the same. For example:
  *Plans for today?* or *So … today?*
- The learners do the same with the rest of the dialogue. They can't change or add words, only remove. The more the better – but they have to keep the original meaning.
- When they have finished, ask them to work in pairs and compare their new versions of the dialogue.
- Each pair writes up a version of the dialogue that they agree upon.
- Bring the class together, and selected pairs or volunteers present their dialogues to practise intonation.

### Possibilities
■ ■ ■ This activity works really well when the dialogue is put into Word format and is projected onto a screen. Individual learners come up to the keyboard, propose changes and the class have to decide whether to accept the changes – or not. (You can do this on a whiteboard too – but it is less elegant.)

■ ■ ■ Each pair can work with a *different* coursebook dialogue which has already been done in class. When the reduced versions are ready, they are circulated. Other pairs have to identify what the original dialogue was, and try to reconstruct the original 'full' version.

**Connects to**
*Top 20 words* (86) ▪ *Howzaboutit?* (76)

## Expansion

Coursebook dialogues are often stilted because their main aim is to practise grammar rather than show features of spoken English. This activity asks the learner to add chunks (*heads* and *tails* – see below) to a dialogue to look after their listener, listen actively or 'hedge' – all important features of spoken grammar.

Level ■ ■ ■    Duration ● ○ ☽

### Preparation
Select a suitable coursebook dialogue – either one that is new to the learners or one that needs reviewing.

### Procedure
- Show the learners the dialogue you have selected and copy the first line onto the board. For example:
  *It's a beautiful day. How about going for a walk?*
- Ask the learners to expand the line by adding chunks.
- Emphasise that the message has to remain more or less the same. For example:
  *It's a beautiful day, **isn't it? A bit of exercise?** How about going for a walk, **you and me**?*
- Get the learners to note that chunks can be added *before* or *after* as a 'head' or a 'tail'.
- The learners work in pairs on the rest of the dialogue, writing it down as they go.
- When they have finished, ask them to display their versions of the dialogue on the walls.
- The pairs mingle and read their different versions of the dialogue aloud to each other to practise their intonation.

### Possibilities
The activity works especially well when the dialogue is in Word format and is projected onto a screen. Individual learners come up to the keyboard and propose changes so the class can decide whether to accept them.

**Connects to**
*Chunks in novels* (76) ▪ *Creative chunks* (60)

# Shadow thinking

This simple drama activity asks the learners to be inventive by providing the thoughts behind the content of a dialogue. The 'shadow thoughts' lend themselves to ellipsis and chunking – they need to be short and to the point because they are elaborating on the original utterance.

Level    Duration

## Preparation
The learners need copies of a dialogue which has two clearly defined roles – see the example below.

## Procedure
- Put the learners into groups of four and give them copies of your dialogue.
- Ask them to choose roles:
  - Two learners sit facing each other, and read the dialogue. (A and B)
  - Each of them is 'shadowed' by another learner, who sits behind them and listens. (C and D)

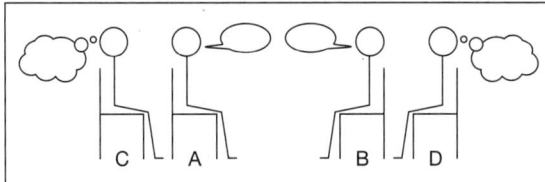

- Now ask the 'shadows' to suggest a parallel dialogue which represents the real thoughts of the speakers. (The other two in the group can help, too.)
- They write down their ideas.
- Below is an example of what one group of our learners came up with:

- When the groups have written their 'shadow dialogues', tell them they are going to perform them. Give them some rehearsal time.
  - The first learner says the first line. (A)
  - Their shadow (C) gives the first thought.
  - The second learner replies. (B)
  - Their shadow (D) gives the thought, and so on.
- When they are ready, arrange two chairs facing each other in front of the class for the learners reading the original dialogue to sit on. Their respective shadows stand behind them.

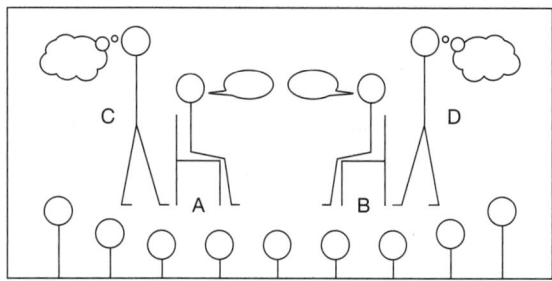

- Each group performs their dialogue in turn.

## Possibilities
Some classes like to make this lightly competitive and have a vote on who created the best dialogue.

We have also videoed classes doing the dialogues – and they have really enjoyed seeing how they performed.

| Dialogue between father-in-law (A) and daughter-in-law (B) | |
|---|---|
| **Original dialogue** | **Shadow thoughts** |
| **A:** Hello, my dear. | **C:** *Oh no, little miss stupid.* |
| **B:** Hello. Nice to see you again. | **D:** *This is going to be difficult.* |
| **A:** We know you're having a difficult time. | **C:** *Not surprised, married to that son of mine.* |
| **B:** Yes, it's sad but …… | **D:** *What's coming now?* |
| **A:** You'll always be a part of the family. | **C:** *She doesn't deserve an idiot like my son.* |
| **B:** You've always been so kind to me. | **D:** *Part of a mad house, you mean.* |

**Connects to**
*Reduction* (46) ▪ *Dense dialogues* (58)

## Chunk for chunk

The aim of this text-based activity is to make the learners realise that the same meaning can be expressed through different chunks. This is a kind of 'translation' exercise – within the same language. The outcomes may also lead to a discussion on register.

Level    Duration ● ● ○

### Preparation
Select a suitable text from the coursebook. (A listening text works best.)

### Procedure
- Pair the learners and tell them they will be writing their own text, based on a coursebook text.
  - They can make any changes they want to the original text.
  - They have to replace 'chunk for chunk'.
- Encourage them to replace chunks with ones that are quite different from the original ones. For example:
  *iron your trousers* – press your pants
  *requires little attention* – is low maintenance
  *lose interest in* – grow tired of
  *grow in confidence* – overcome shyness

  Discourage changes like '*hoover the carpet* – shampoo the rug', which change the meaning.
- Display the learners' new texts so they can mingle and compare the various versions.
- Finally, they look at their new texts and try to reconstruct the original aloud.

### Possibilities
■ ■ ■ Some texts lend themselves to concentrating the learners' attention on a specific area. So if there are lots of time references, you can ask the learners to focus on them:
two days ago – *the day before yesterday*
about 22 – *more or less my sister's age*
in the last decade – *less than ten years ago*

You can select similar texts from the coursebook, for example three short texts around a theme or biographies. The learners choose one text per pair and keep it a secret. Then they re-write it, replacing chunks. Display the new texts – the others identify which text was the inspiration for the new text and try to remember the original chunks.

You can choose a text about the capital/regions of countries: the learners re-write it so that it is true for *them*.

**Connects to**
*Skilful monologue* (61)

## L1–L2 translation

Translating from L1 to L2, and vice-versa, helps learners realise that chunks are often very different in their concept; for example, in Polish, *take photos* is 'make photos'; *keep my fingers crossed* is 'hold my thumbs'.

Level    Duration ● ● ◡

### Preparation
Select 10–15 chunks from a text you have recently worked on in the coursebook. Translate the chunks into the learners' native language. If you want to, you can prepare a handout; the translation of the English chunks should be in the same order as they appear in the text.

### Procedure
- Dictate the translations of the chunks to the class, or distribute the handout with the chunks you have selected.
  - The learners work in pairs and translate them into English.
  - If they cannot translate the chunk, they leave the space blank.
- Put two pairs together to compare their results.
- The learners open their books and look at the text where the chunks came from:
  - They find the originals.
  - They compare the translations they have come up with.
- Discuss any problems, focusing on accuracy in producing chunks and concentrating on the 'small' words.
  For example:
  *come to light* vs *come to the light*
  *rings a bell* vs *rings the bell*

### Possibilities
The above activity works differently in different languages – so use your knowledge of the learners' L1 to select the most challenging ones for *your* learners.

**Connects to**
*Film titles* (80) ▪ *Translate that!* (40)

## Mischunking

When reading, misunderstanding may be due to 'mischunking'. Correct chunking – noticing where chunks begin and end – is important, especially when reading aloud. As the learners read, they will become more aware of reading out chunks as units and using link-ups and primary and secondary stress.

Level ▫■■   Duration ●●◡

### Preparation
Prepare a handout with fragments of sentences, or whole sentences which have potential for mischunking. Ideally, create a bank of these examples from your class when your learners make *real* mistakes while reading aloud from the coursebook.

### Procedure
- Write a sentence like the following on the board:
  *In addition to this Brazil has the most beautiful stadium.*

- Show how a learner could read it aloud wrongly, and how it *should* be read:
  *In addition to this Brazil / has the most beautiful stadium.* Wrong
  *In addition to this / Brazil has the most beautiful stadium.* Correct

  *It was a long hike up / the mountain.* Wrong
  *It was a long hike / up the mountain.* Correct

- Give out the sentences you have collected and ask the learners to decide how each of the examples can be mischunked, and how they should be read correctly.

- Encourage the learners to put in a slash (/) where one chunk ends and a new one starts.

- Practise reading aloud with the whole class and discuss the problems involved.

### Possibilities
It is possible to follow this up by starting an ongoing project in which the learners collect and pool similar examples themselves.

When learners read aloud, it is easy for the teacher to diagnose problems with chunking. So it may be useful to revise the importance of reading aloud as a technique that has undeservedly fallen into disrepute.

**Connects to**
*Chunks in the news* (74) ▪ *How many words?* (30)

## Building around a chunk

This activity raises awareness of where chunks begin and end, and also makes the learners aware of the varying length of chunks. It is useful preparation for gap-fill and multiple-choice exercises and exam tasks.

Level ■■■   Duration ●●◡

### Preparation
Look through the coursebook and find a set of longish chunks which all have the same key word. (In the samples below, we have chosen the prepositions *at* and *to*.) Cut down the chunks so that they all begin (or end) with the key word.

### Procedure
- Give out your copies or write up the reduced chunks, and ask the learners to expand the chunks by adding words.

  > **Lower level**
  > Reduced chunks: *at university / at noon / at French*
  > Original chunks: *study at university / at noon sharp / be good at French*
  > **Higher level**
  > Reduced chunks: *to my mind / to going there / to have forgotten*
  > Original chunks: *came to my mind / look forward to going there / seems to have forgotten*

- Discuss the suggestions with the whole class:
  - They don't need to reproduce the original chunks.
  - You eliminate the sentences which are not likely combinations of words.

- For further practice, ask the learners to write sentences or a text in which their chunks are in context. They don't need to use all of them.

- Monitor as they write, then circulate or exhibit what they have produced for the other learners to see.

### Possibilities
This activity can be adapted to practise phrasal verbs that are introduced in the coursebook. You give the learners the phrasal verb 'make up' and they look up, or come up with, extended chunks in which it appears, eg *make up before a party*, *kiss and make up*, *make up a story*. They then write a short text in which the three chunks appear naturally. (Phrasal verbs are hard to learn or retain unless they are contextualised in a likely chunk.)

You can use this technique to get the learners to prepare multiple-choice grammar questions.

**Connects to**
*Chunks first, then grammar* (50) ▪ *Grammar from chunks* (60)

# Chunks first, then grammar

Starting with a key word, the learners build up chunks, finally adding the grammar. This sequence is probably how our brain works, which means that when coursebooks present and practise grammar and *then* add the lexis they are 'back to front'. This is a useful preparation for speaking and writing activities.

**Level** ▫ ■ ■    **Duration** ● ● ○

## Preparation
Choose a key word around a theme. This activity works well if it is the theme of a unit of the coursebook. See below for an example with the word 'relationship'.

## Procedure
- Write the key word on the board and ask the learners, working alone, to come up with five *adjectives* which are *likely* to go before. (Emphasise the 'likely' and give a context if necessary, ie a personal relationship, not a business relationship.)
- After the learners have had time to think, brainstorm their suggestions to the board. You might get:

  stormy
  casual
  sexual          relationship
  three-year
  easy-going

- Reject adjectives which you or they consider 'unlikely'.
- Now give the learners some time to come up with a few *verbs* that are likely.
- Brainstorm again, rejecting or accepting:

  have            stormy
  be in           casual
  enjoy           sexual          relationship
  want            three-year
  be involved in  easy-going

- Finally, ask the learners to add the grammar to the chunks. Write the following model on the board:
  Subject + verb + article (or possessive adjective) + relationship + adverbial
- Give them a bit of time to come up with a few examples:
  *They started a stormy relationship in the summer.*
  *After being married they now had a number of casual relationships for a change.*
- Check in groups and help as necessary.

## Possibilities
You can ask the learners to keep their list of chunks (verb + adjective + noun) at the ready for subsequent writing or speaking activities. This will help them select the appropriate ready-made chunks and also give them more time to think about the appropriate grammar to go with the chunks.

If you have access to good corpus-based dictionaries and/or the internet in class, the learners can check and add to their 'verb + adjective + noun' combinations. This can be a good homework task.

■ ▫ ▫ With elementary coursebooks, there is usually a unit on appearance. Choose the key words *hair* or *clothes*, and follow the procedure above. The result might be:

Subject + verb + article/possessive + adjective + *hair* + adverbial
*He combed his curly hair again.*
*She straightened her hair before going to the party.*

This sentence-building is also a very useful task when *designing* reading tasks. Simply select the key word(s) in the text and do the sentence-building as a pre- or post-reading activity.

**Connects to**
*Word sketch* (95) ▪ *Grammar from chunks* (60)

## Everything is right

This activity encourages the learners to give their own answers and context, in addition to the 'correct' answer in the coursebook. Correct answers to exercises are dependent on the context to a given example, but nearly always the coursebook fails to give *enough* context and learners often notice this.

Level    Duration

### Preparation
Select a matching exercise from the coursebook and have copies ready for each learner, or refer them directly to the coursebook.

### Procedure
- Give out your matching exercise and ask the learners to do it, working alone. Our sample opposite is at upper-intermediate level.
- The learners check, using the key in the coursebook.
- Now point out that the answers given by the book are the most 'likely' answers – but that others are possible.
- Set the task again. This time, ask the learners to come up with another match which is acceptable for each question.
- When they have a second answer, put them into pairs and get them to test each other. The pairs will need to provide a context in which the new answer makes sense. (You monitor and arbitrate as necessary.)

### Possibilities
You can set up the activity as a competition, with the learners working in pairs or small groups. Have a scoring system:
- 1 point for the coursebook answer
- 2 points for an alternative answer
- 4 points for any subsequent alternative answer

To score the extra points, the learners must be able to contextualise and justify their answer in a way that is accepted by the rest of the class – and by you.

This variation may sound far-fetched, but we have done it in class and the learners like to be stretched like this:
- Divide the class into eight groups and give each group *one* question each – but *all eight* possible answers.
- They have to make all eight answers possible.
- Make a new group of eight, one learner from each group.
- They justify their answers and give contexts to make them clear to the other seven.

---

**Match the following sentences:**
1) I'd like them if you can get them.
2) Why don't you do it?
3) Would you like a cup of coffee?
4) You made me look ridiculous there.

a) Not just now, thanks.
b) Well, I'll just ring and ask someone to bring them, then.
c) I looked just as ridiculous as you did.
d) It's just not done.

---

The correct responses given by the book were:
1 – b, 2 – d, 3 – a, 4 – c.
(Since the responses are authentic examples taken from a corpus, they are also the responses that happened in real life.)

But here is just one example of what learners can come up with:

Why don't you do it? Not just now, thanks.
ie *Don't bring that up again.*

Why don't you do it? I'd like them if you can get them.
ie *OK, I agree to your plan/suggestion.*

Why don't you do it? I looked as ridiculous as you did.
ie *I've done it already so don't need to do it again.*

---

**Connects to**
*Tolerating ambiguity* (52)

## Tolerating ambiguity

Coursebook exercises have one fixed answer. But learners often think 'outside the box', and this activity encourages them to come up with *more* answers. Changing the instruction from 'correct the word order' to 'give more than one meaning to the utterance' gets the learners to give meaning to language.

Level ▯ ■ ■     Duration ● ● ◡

### Preparation
Find an exercise in the coursebook where the instruction asks the learners to correct the word order in a sentence.

### Procedure
▪ Give out copies of the exercise to the learners, or refer them to the exercise in the coursebook. Our example is at upper-intermediate level:

> **Correct these sentences:**
> a) You'll have I think to have your hair cut.
> b) These days in a car it's not far to drive.
> c) French I studied in Paris in a language school.
> d) Quietly I've been today sitting in the sun.

▪ Ask the learners to change the instruction at the top of the page:
  - They cross out 'Correct these sentences'.
  - They change to '*Change the word order of the following sentences to get a correct sentence. Do this twice with each sentence.*'

▪ They work in pairs or on their own, completing the exercise by following the new instructions. If they get *more* than two answers per question, so much the better!

▪ Finally, check their answers by getting them to read them out aloud.

### Possibilities
▯ ■ ■ You can give a different instruction: '*Do not change the word order in the original text, but work on intonation and imagine a context in which the sentences would be correct.*' To do this, the learners need to split the sentences into chunks. After they have had enough time, they test their ideas by reading aloud. This stretches them and makes the activity more challenging.

**Connects to**
*Your last chance* (96)

## A word or a phrase?

Exercises meant to practise spoken English in the coursebook are often stiff, formal and more like written English. A simple change in the instructions turns them into a real test of spoken English. The learners become aware of the importance of intonation and lexical density to give meaning to spoken utterances.

Level ▯ ■ ■     Duration ● ● ●

### Preparation
Find a gap-fill exercise in the coursebook where the instruction asks the learners to fill in the gaps with a word or phrase.

### Procedure
▪ Give out copies of the exercise, or refer the learners to the coursebook. For example:

> **Fill in the gaps with a suitable word or phrase.**
> No, I ____ ____ ____ next Friday
> ____ ____ next week?
> No, next week ____ ____ good, either.
> When ____ ____ ____ ____ ?
> Don't know. Look, I'm ____ ____ now. Must rush.

▪ Ask the learners to change the instruction at the top of the page:
  - They cross out 'or phrase', leaving the instruction as 'a suitable word'.
  - They complete the exercise, but they can only use *one word* to fill each gap.

▪ Finally, get them to read their answers aloud – there is usually more than one answer.

> **The answers in the book were:**
> *can't make it / What about / is no / can you make it / really busy*
> **One-word answers suggested by our learners:**
> *can't / try / no / then / off*

### Possibilities
■ ■ ■ You can repeat the activity, asking the learners to see how many of the utterances they can make meaningful by changing just the intonation – without adding any words.

Some learners are prey to 'creative misunderstanding': one of our learners misread the instructions and so came up with this activity.

**Connects to**
*Your last chance* (96)

## Tests with a twist

The learners work on the chunks associated with the *answers* to multiple-choice questions before attempting the *question* – increasing their understanding of how a multiple-choice exercise works in order to improve exam performance.

Level ▫■■    Duration ●●○

### Preparation
Select a multiple-choice vocabulary exercise for your learners' level.

### Procedure
- Write the choice of answers for the first question on the board. For example:

    A. place    B. world    C. earth    D. space

- In pairs, the learners try to predict what chunks the words might appear in. Invite them to think of at least two or three possibilities for each word. They are to think of *chunks*, not *other words* built from the word – 'out of this world' rather than 'worldwide'.

- Write their suggestions on the board and discuss them with the whole class. Eliminate expressions which are not likely combinations of words.

- Now write the original gapped sentence on the board. The learners complete it using one of the four options. For example:

    *It opened up his eyes to a whole new _____ .*

- See if they have anticipated the 'correct' chunk. For 'world', our learners once came up with:

    a world of imagination      all over the word
    he means the world to me    out of this world
    worlds apart                come into the world

- Discuss why *place/world/earth/space* have been put together in the example question, and to what extent chunks containing these words can be confusing.

- Continue with a few more test items and repeat the procedure until the learners have grasped the importance of chunking for choosing the correct options, then finish the exercise in the normal way.

### Possibilities
This activity can also be used with many multiple cloze tests which appear in some exams.

**Connects to**
*Building around a chunk* (49)

## Gaps with a twist

Learners may know a high-frequency word, yet be unaware of how many chunks it is 'involved' with. This activity provides strategies and training for 'gapped sentence' tasks in exams.

Level ▫■▫    Duration ●●●

### Preparation
Select some key words from the units of the coursebook you have already covered. Prepare some slips of paper, big enough to write three sentences on.

### Procedure
- Put the learners into pairs and give a different key word to each of the pairs.
    - They look through their books and find chunks with their word.
    - They copy three different sentences, but leave out the key word.

- In the example, the learners have left out the word 'one':

    > I was there at _____ o'clock.
    > You don't need any more helpers. This is a _____-man job.
    > She had some problems with her English so now she has some _____-to-_____ lessons.

- The sentences circulate, and other pairs guess the word, keeping a separate record of their answers.

- When all the slips of paper have circulated, stop the activity and discuss the answers.

### Possibilities
▫■▫ If the learners cannot guess the word, they can skim through the coursebook to find the answer. This makes the activity a little easier and encourages skim reading.

The pairs can give extra clues about where to find the chunks, eg by giving the unit or the page number where to find them.

Instead of *you* selecting the key words, the learners can skim the coursebook and select their own.

▫▫■ You can do this kind of activity specifically as a strategy to prepare for exams such as the ESOL CAE and CPE. Recycling language from the coursebook and helping learners to memorise chunks is good preparation for successful exam performance. By writing their own exam questions, they develop insights into how the exam works.

**Connects to**
*Gapped sentences DIY* (54)

53

# Gapped sentences DIY

This activity gets the learners designing their own 'gapped sentences' exam tasks to test their peers and making them aware of the importance of lexical chunking in the design of the exams they will have to do.

**Level** ❑ ■ ■      **Duration** ● ● ○

## Preparation
Prepare a handout with gapped sentences (see the sample below). You will also need sets of corpus-based dictionaries or internet access to online dictionaries.

## Procedure
- Ask the learners to pool chunks with the word 'red' and write them on the board. For example (at higher levels):

| | | | |
|---|---|---|---|
| red tape | see red | paint the town red | go red |
| red hair | red wine | red letter day | Red Army |
| be in the red | red card | red car | red alert |
| like a red rag to a bull | | roll out the red carpet | |

- In pairs, the learners choose a couple of chunks from the list and write a sentence for each.
- Discuss the sentences they have written and how easy it would be to guess the key word if it was removed – and why.
- Distribute the handout you have prepared (see the example below) and ask the pairs to do the task. They can use dictionaries.

> 1 The _____ between the boat and the pier was a tricky one.
> If you get access to the paintings, _____ at the chance to see them.
> Be careful. Don't _____ in with both feet.
> 2 Despite the cold _____, a white Christmas was an unlikely prospect for most people.
> Employers should avoid making _____ decisions in cases of sickness absence.
> Seeing the car as its territory, the dog may attempt to _____ fiercely at them.

- Discuss the answers (*jump* for the first example, *snap* for the second) with the learners:
  - They should observe that the three sentences in a set are not necessarily of the same difficulty.
  - They should rank them from the easiest to most difficult, in their opinion.
- Discuss the answers, then refer the pairs to the list on the board and ask them to choose three uses of the word *red*:
  - One they think is quite easy
  - One difficult
  - One very difficult
- Discuss the answers, then give out the dictionaries, asking each pair to choose a word and prepare a gapped-sentence exam task containing three sentences. (See *Gaps with a twist*.)
- If possible, make sure each group has a different key word.
- Remind them to choose examples of varying degrees of difficulty:
  - One they *expect* their colleagues to know
  - One they *might* know
  - One they expect them *not* to know
- Monitor, help and check they understand the task. When the sets of three sentences are ready, ask the learners to copy them with the key word removed.
- Circulate the sets and get the learners to work out each other's answers.
- End with a plenary discussion on the process and the intention of the examiner.

## Possibilities
If you teach a number of classes at the same level, you can ask one class to prepare the task for another. It can develop into a competitive challenge to motivate tired exam classes.

❑ ❑ ■ It will also help the learners prepare for some exams (eg CAE or CPE) which include tasks where the key word in three sentences has been removed from the chunk and they have to find the word.

Examples of such tasks are available on the internet – the learners can google 'gapped sentences' to get more. They can easily get authentic examples for their gapped sentences from Google, too.

We took our examples from the British National Corpus. The first set is authentic but modified by the authors; the second is authentic. The learners can use the simple search facility in the BNC to research their key word themselves and come up with three typical uses to test their peers. (See Chapter Five for more on the BNC.)

**Connects to**
*Gaps with a twist* (53)

# Chapter Three
## In action

This chapter contains tried and tested activities to consolidate and build the learners' confidence when using chunks. Once they have a knowledge of chunks, learners need time and experience to escape the tyranny of trying to be correct. They need to experiment: 'likely' or 'unlikely' is a good response, as is 'It depends'. The more the learners experience, the more they can tolerate ambiguity and develop their own inner criteria.

Many of the activities can be done at lower levels, but there is more emphasis on higher levels in this chapter. The second half of the chapter deals with the more cultural aspects of chunks – Where are they used? and What for? There is also an emphasis on spoken English.

## Practice
The first activities revise and consolidate the ideas of chunking presented in the previous chapters. These are followed by a series of activities which concentrate on fluency in spoken English.

## Priming
The next three activities are about priming meaning in chunks – distinguishing what meaning they have been assigned by use in the speech community.

## Pragmatics
Chunks also have a pragmatic meaning – they are used for language play, for bonding within a group, for politeness. These are mainly speaking activities and they have a cultural component which will therefore stretch higher-level learners.

---

### The class blues

In this first activity, the learners play with chunks of various lengths, focusing on stress, intonation and the pronunciation of words in the stressed and unstressed positions within a chunk.

Level ■ ■ ■    Duration ● ● ◡

#### Preparation
Prepare lots of slips of paper. (If you have a learner who plays the guitar, ask them to bring it to class.)

#### Procedure
- Tell the learners that they are going to write a 'class blues' and that each line has to follow the same pattern:

    *This blues is a _____ blues.*

- Divide the class into pairs and give out three slips of paper per pair.
- Each pair writes two or three lines of the blues, each on a separate slip. Make the following clear:
  - The number of words in each gap is up to each pair.
  - The number of words can differ from line to line.
- Give an example. This is a sample from our learners:

> *This blues is a miss you blues.*
> *This blues is a nothing to write home about blues.*
> *This blues is a nothing to wear blues.*
> *This blues is a my mother is angry with me blues.*

- The learners pool the lines:
  - They arrange the slips in the order they prefer.
  - They then write them on the board.
- The class sing the blues.
- They all sing as one group, or each pair sings their lines, accompanied by the class guitarist if you have one.

#### Possibilities
If nobody plays the guitar, the learners can just clap or tap the blues beat.

If you have an overhead projector, it is quicker than using the board. Write the lyrics on an OHP transparency and project them.

---

**Connects to**
*Songs in your head* (79)

# A 'likely' wife

This activity asks the learners to build bigger and bigger chunks around a key word, making them aware of how long a noun phrase/chunk can be (normally up to seven words or so).

Level ⌟ ■ ■    Duration ● ● ⌡

## Procedure

- Tell the learners the activity they are going to do is about making phrases longer and longer.

- Give them a pattern, for example:
    a _____ wife

- Invite suggestions as to what the missing adjective could be and ask them to extend it; here are some examples from our learners:

| a lovable wife | a plain wife | a rejected wife |
| a beautiful wife | an ordinary wife | a jealous wife |

- Ask the learners to expand the chunk still further by adding nouns, prepositions, etc.
    a _____ _____ wife

- Then pairs try to think of more possibilities:
    a ___ ___ ___ wife
    a ___ ___ ___ ___ wife
    a ___ ___ ___ ___ ___ wife
    a ___ ___ ___ ___ ___ ___ wife

- Discuss the various possibilities the learners have come up with. Reject 'impossible' phrases or suggestions like *A car arrived and took away his wife* which are sentences rather than chunks.

- Here are some of the suggestions our learners thought of:

    an immensely inquisitive wife
    a very inquisitive wife
    a terribly inquisitive wife
    an awfully untidy wife
    an extremely good looking wife
    a spoilt unfaithful ex-wife
    a stay at home wife
    a good looking and hard working wife
    a rather stubborn but orderly and lovable wife
    a stay at home with the kids wife

- Ask the learners to pronounce each of the phrases – and to observe how more and more *condensed* the phrases become, in order to fit into one beat.

## Possibilities

You could use 'husband' – but the results would not be so interesting, and it might be a case of political correctness gone mad. The derogatory results of coming up with chunks with 'wife' are probably inevitable – they reflect the language and the learners' knowledge of the language. We need to examine *connotation* in a technical way – which is not the same as agreeing with the social and cultural bias inherent in the language.

There is a question about how one would write some of the chunks listed above. Is it a hyphenated *stay-at-home wife* (to reflect the condensed pronunciation) or *stay at home wife*? There is no definitive answer, so if your learners are interested, you can ask them to research on the Web and see if they can get a representative sample.

If you get a similar list from native speakers to show your learners, they will enjoy comparing their lists with what their 'native' counterparts came up with.

**Connects to**
*Chunk quest* (83)

## Mind the gap

Chunks often sound like one word – *Erase and rewind* sounds like *eraseandrewind* when sung (by The Cardigans). This activity helps learners with their listening strategies, helping them to recognise chunks and the different lengths of chunks.

Level ■ ■ ■    Duration ● ● ◡

### Preparation
Choose a song suitable for the age and level of your class that is not too well-known. Write the lyrics, with gaps replacing complete chunks of two, three or more words. Prepare one copy per learner.

### Procedure
- Give out the worksheets you have prepared and ask the learners to work in pairs:
    - They try to predict how many words have been removed in each gap.
    - They don't have to predict what the words are.
    - They compare their predictions with another pair.
- Play the song twice.
- Working individually, the learners write down how many words have been removed.
- In their original pairs, they compare their notes and discuss their predictions.
- Play the song again and, this time, the learners complete the lyrics.
- Discuss the answers with the whole class.

### Possibilities
Instead of simply predicting the number of words missing, the learners can predict what the missing chunk is in the first stage of the activity – if you select a song which is relatively easy for the class.

Instead of songs, you can use podcasts, from, for example, *http://www.guardian.co.uk/*. Prepare a handout with the transcript of the text with gaps – and then follow the procedure above.

**Connects to**
*Kiss the sky* (78) ▪ *Howzaboutit?* (76)

## 7–1 dialogues

This activity encourages fluent speaking through writing. It is very artificial – but with natural results, mirroring the pattern of real spoken grammar. As a conversation develops and knowledge is shared, *lexical density* becomes a feature – less grammar and more chunks.

Level ■ ■ ■    Duration ● ● ◡

### Procedure
- Draw the following on the board:

    ___ ___ ___ ___ ___ ___ ___
    ___ ___ ___ ___ ___ ___
    ___ ___ ___ ___ ___
    ___ ___ ___ ___
    ___ ___ ___
    ___ ___
    ___

- Pair the learners and ask them to write a dialogue following the pattern – the first utterance has *seven* words, the second *six* – and so on, down to *one*.
- When they have finished, they read aloud their dialogues to other pairs or to the whole class:
    - What are you going to do tonight?
    - I'm going to see a film?
    - Which film and what time?
    - Harry Potter, at seven.
    - Can I come?
    - Of course.
    - Great.

### Possibilities
■ ■ ■ A useful follow-up is an **A-Z**. This time, the restriction is that, starting with A, each line of the dialogue must start with the next letter of the alphabet. An example:
- **A**nn, hi.
- **B**e careful. There's a big dog beside you.
- **C**at?
- **D**og, not cat.
- **E**xactly. I like dogs.
    **F**ine. Take him home. I think he's lost.
- **G**reat idea.

As the conversation develops, *ellipsis* becomes a feature. The learners write a dialogue in pairs then they circulate them from pair to pair, or present them to the whole class. If they read them out, allow some time for rehearsal and work on intonation. (Mario Rinvolucri originally came up with this type of activity.)

**Connects to**
*One-word conversations* (31) ▪ *Recycling a dialogue* (45)

## Dense dialogues

This is a drama-based activity to get the learners using lexical density and incompleteness or ellipsis, rather than full grammatical sentences when speaking. It also encourages them to listen to each other very carefully.

Level ■ ■ ■     Duration ● ◡ ◡

### Procedure

- Put the learners into threes, sitting comfortably in as much space as possible.
- They need to decide on two speakers and a 'controller':
  - The speakers sit opposite each other.
  - The controller sits to one side.
- The learners decide which of the two speakers goes first.
- The controller says a number, from 1–5.
  - If it is '5', the first speaker restricts their utterance to that number of words:
    *How is it going, then?*
  - The controller gives another number.
  - If it is '3', the second learner replies in three words:
    *Fine thanks. You?*
- Continue for 90 seconds, or until the learners have had a reasonable conversation.
- Repeat the procedure twice, so that all the learners get the chance to be the controller.

### Possibilities

The controller can also specify the speaker. So, instead of the AB / AB pattern, the controller varies the *turn-taking* as well as the number of words in each utterance:
AB / AA / BA / BB, etc.
(Most coursebook dialogues are AB / AB, which is unnatural.)

Instead of giving the *limit* of words, the controller can say a *word* that the speaker has to use, forcing them to think of appropriate chunks.

The activity (which we learned from Action Theatre, based in Vienna) can be done in pairs, with dice instead of a controller.

**Connects to**
*Reduction* (46) • *Recycling a dialogue* (45)

## Conversation countdown

This is a fluency activity which encourages the learners to work on lexical density, ellipsis and incompleteness in spoken English.

Level ■ ■ ■     Duration ● ◡ ◡

### Preparation

You need a clock or watch with a second hand.

### Procedure

- Invite two volunteers to the front of the class, and get them sitting comfortably.
- Give them a topic, and 90 seconds to have a conversation.
- Ask the class to listen very carefully.
- Invite two more volunteers to repeat the conversation as far as possible but, this time, give them 60 seconds.
- Make it clear that the activity is not about speaking *faster* but about *eliminating* unnecessary bits of language.
- Repeat the procedure, reducing the time to 45, 30 and, finally, to 15 seconds.
- Discuss with the learners which dialogues sounded more natural, and why.

### Possibilities

You could record the dialogues for further work, but this could inhibit the learners.

To ease the possible pressure in the activity, it can be done in pairs, rather than in front of the whole class, and the learners can be given time to rehearse and improve the dialogues.

**Connects to**
*Gossip, not communication* (65) • *7–1 dialogues* (57)

PRACTICE    CHAPTER 3    PRACTICE

## Incomplete grammar

This activity practises 'incompleteness' in chunks when speaking – encouraging chunking rather than using full sentences. It also involves intonation practice for the learners.

Level    Duration ● ● ◡

### Preparation
You need a bag full of building blocks of different colours. Cuisenaire rods are good, but anything will do – we have used paper clips or buttons. The important thing is to have a *variety* of colours and sizes.

### Procedure
- Build a sentence using the blocks, with each part of speech represented by a different colour. The *choice* of code for the colours is not important – as long as it is *consistent*.

- The code established here is shown in Example 1 below. Get the learners to memorise it:

    pronoun     = *orange*
    verb        = *red*
    preposition = *black*
    article     = *blue*
    noun        = *green*
    conjunction = *pink*
    adjective   = *yellow*

- The blocks in Example 1 represent:

    'We went to the lake and had a good swim.'

- You repeat the sentence a few times (don't write it down) for the learners to repeat – until they learn the sentence by heart. Leave the blocks where they are, to aid memory.

- As a quick test, ask the learners what colour a *verb* is, what colour a *noun*, an *article*, etc.

- Remember: the choice of colour code does not matter too much, as long as it is clearly established.

- Pair the learners and ask them to take eight blocks out of the bag – without looking.
    - Each pair constructs a sentence using only those parts of speech represented by the blocks they have selected.
    - If they have forgotten the code, refer them back to your example.

- The learners then show the blocks which represent their sentence and 'read' it aloud for the class. For example:

    A pair who selected three green blocks (*nouns*), three pink ones (*conjunctions*), one yellow (*adjective*) and one red (*verb*) might come up with Example 2:

    'Mary … and … and … and John find swimming enjoyable.'

    Or they might come up with Example 3:

    'But … but … driver or passenger are hurt … Ambulance!'

### Possibilities
■ ■ ◡ At lower levels, the learners can take eight blocks but don't need to use *all* of them.

You can use this activity (invented by Tadeusz Wolańczuk) to encourage the learners to give *meaning* to language – 'probabilistic grammar' rather than 'deterministic grammar' (with *subject*, *verb* and *object*).

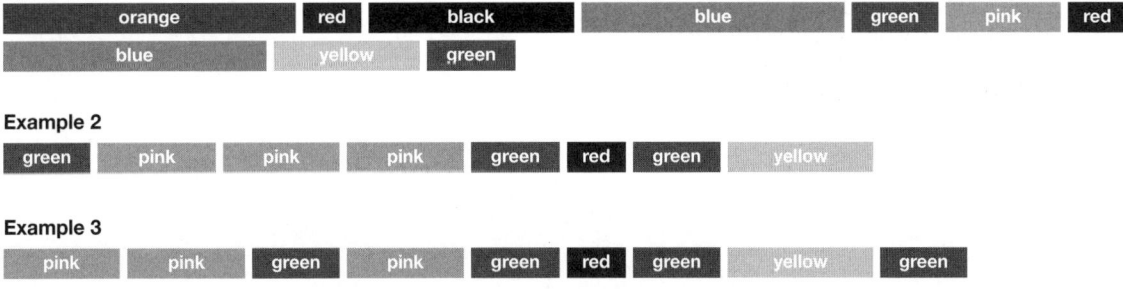

**Connects to**
*Creative chunks* (60) ▪ *Recycling a dialogue* (45)

## Grammar from chunks

The learners build chunks around a noun – before adding the grammar – to make a sentence. This can be a preparation for extended speaking or writing around a specific theme suggested by the key word.

Level ▁ ■ ■    Duration ● ● ○

### Preparation
Select a noun which is an important key word for your learners, or linked to a theme/unit of the coursebook. Dictionaries will also be useful.

### Procedure
- Write the following on the board, writing the key word in the middle column and the other words either side:

  *Subject | verb | adj. |* **noun** *| preposition | object | adv.*
  *operation*

- Working in pairs, ask the learners to construct realistic sentences with likely word partnerships.
- Monitor and consult as necessary, helping the learners to work on the most likely combinations of words.
- The learners write their sentence on the board or they exchange them across pairs.
- This is an example of what our learners came up with (with the teacher's help and dictionaries when necessary):

  > *The team carried out/did an emergency operation on the crash victim in the downstairs theatre.*
  >
  > *The patient had a routine operation on his cyst in the surgery.*

### Possibilities
Tell the learners to keep their sentences. They will be very useful preparation and models for a subsequent speaking or extended-writing activity.

The version above is ESP-orientated, used with trainee doctors we were teaching. It is obviously applicable to other ESP/EAP situations, depending on the key word(s) you choose and the interests of the learners.

## Creative chunks

This activity focuses on how a simple sentence and a small pool of words can lead to the creation of a variety of chunks. By restricting the words, the learners are forced to be creative.

Level ▁ ■ ■    Duration ● ● ◗

### Preparation
Select a suitable sentence which lends itself to the activity (see the example below).

### Procedure
- Write the key sentence on the board:

  *I am so happy. I like my work but I work too much.*

- Ask the learners to use the words in the sentence to generate new utterances. For example:

  > *I so like my work. Too much, but I am happy.*
  > *I work, like, too much. Am I happy too?*
  > *I am my work. But too much? I like work. Happy?*

- Allow some time, but emphasise that the learners should try to use *most* or *all* the words – but no added ones – and that punctuation can be used freely.
- Invite suggestions from the class and write them on the board.
- The learners read their lines aloud. Emphasise the importance of appropriate intonation.

### Possibilities
For a wonderful example of playful poetry which perfectly illustrates the rationale behind the activity above, you can send them (or, even better, accompany them) to the following website where you will find *The Uncertainty of the Poet* by Wendy Cope, published in 1992 by Faber and Faber:
*http://www.cs.rice.edu/~ssiyer/minstrels/poems/1499.html*

---

**Connects to**
*Word sketch* (95) ▪ *From chunks to sentences* (90)

**Connects to**
*Incomplete grammar* (59) ▪ *Recycling a dialogue* (45)

# Skilful monologue

The learners are encouraged to activate chunks they already know but tend momentarily to forget, while at the same time expanding their range of expression and improving their speaking skills.

Level    Duration

## Procedure

- Suggest a topic such as *Life in the country* and ask a 'reliable' volunteer to speak about it for two minutes – without preparation:
    - The learner speaks for two minutes.
    - The rest of the class just listen.
    - You take notes of some chunks the learner uses.
- Focus on chunks that are *below* the learner's level – ones that do not reflect their mastery of the language and could easily be replaced by more advanced chunks.
- When the learner has spoken for two minutes, stop the monologue and thank the volunteer.
- Write on the board the chunks you have noted down. Emphasise that these are not mistakes. For example:

    | it is obvious | nice views |
    | healthy food | peace and quiet |
    | tasty food | no competition |

- Brainstorm alternative chunks that could substitute for the ones you have selected:

    | it is obvious | – it goes without saying |
    | healthy food | – nutritious ingredients, local produce, organic, free range chickens and eggs |
    | tasty food | – mouth-watering, succulent, a delight to the palate |
    | nice views | – rolling hills, picturesque and breathtaking views |
    | peace and quiet | – tranquillity, silence rings in the ears |
    | no competition | – away from the rat race, no keeping up with the Joneses |

- Invite another volunteer to come forward – and suggest a new topic.
- The learner monologues and, this time, the rest of the class all take notes.
- Finally, they compare their observations, pool their chunks and suggest improved alternatives.

## Possibilities

You can repeat the activity as an ongoing project.

You can record a learner's monologue:
- Play it to the whole class and ask the learners to take notes.
- Discuss the overall impression and invite comments.
- Replay the dialogue, stopping when a learner uses a chunk that could be replaced by a more advanced expression.
- Pool ideas with the class and then continue.
- Repeat the procedure as many times as necessary.

To ease the stress factor, use a monologue that was produced by a learner from another class – an anonymous learner of the same language level.

This activity can also be adapted for improving the learners' use of lexis in writing. Underline expressions that could be expressed in a better, more advanced way. Then the learners come up with, or research, more sophisticated lexis.

You can specifically practise retrieving, using and improving chunks as an exam preparation skill. In language exams, learners have to demonstrate their best spoken language and lexis. Very often, especially in a stressful situation, they tend to forget all the sophisticated lexis they have learnt.

---

**Connects to**
*Chunk for chunk* (48) • *Dictionary versus dictionary* (93)

## Rapid repairs

This activity prepares the learners to be more confident about hesitating and 'repairing' as an aid to keep going when trying to find the appropriate chunk. In essence, they are being encouraged to sort and retrieve – rather than stopping dead when they think they have made a 'mistake'.

**Level** ■ ■ ■   **Duration** ● ● ◡

### Procedure
- Pair the learners and ask each pair to decide who is the speaker and who is the writer.
- Dictate the following stems at speed:
    *I live on ...*
    *I live in ...*
    *I live at ...*
- The speaker is to complete the stems as quickly as possible. The writer has to note down *exactly* what the speaker said, including hesitations and reformulations.
- They might get, for example:
    *I live on ... er ... Westerplatte Street.*
    *I live in a top floor flat.*
    *I live at ... Westerplatte St ... at 36 Westerplatte Street in Sopot.*
- Pause and get them to check for slips and note the reformulations. They can check with you if they are not quite sure.
- Emphasise that when you speak, nobody knows exactly what you intended to say – so you can change your intention while speaking.
- Repeat with:
    *I got there on ...*
    *I got there in ...*
    *I got there at ...*
    *I work on ...*
    *I work in ...*
    *I work at ...*

### Possibilities
While the learners are involved in *any* speaking activity, you can collect examples of sentences that lend themselves to this activity. When you have a few, dictate the beginnings and get the learners to complete – using *their* utterances to improve their repair techniques through activating different chunks.

**Connects to**
*Answers to questions* (28) ▪ *What was the question?* (66)

## Small change, big difference

This activity shows how a small change in the combination of words that make a chunk changes the meaning that the word partnership is 'primed' to convey.

**Level** ■ ■ ■   **Duration** ● ● ◡

### Preparation
Prepare a sample text (see below).

### Procedure
- Write the following quote (from Mae West, Hollywood actress and personality) on the board:
    *It's not the man in your life that's important, it's the life in your man.*
- Check the learners' understanding, then repeat with the following example taken from a sign outside a pub:
    *It's nice to be important but it's more important to be nice.*
- Now give out your sample text (these examples are at upper-intermediate):

    | | |
    |---|---|
    | drinking problem | problem drinking |
    | a cooking pot | a pot cooking |
    | driving mad | mad driving |
    | take over | overtake |
    | a roof slate | a slate roof |
    | open a letter | an open letter |
    | reach out | outreach |
    | up jumped | jumped up |

- In small groups, ask the learners to comment on the differences in meaning. Monitor and help as necessary.

### Possibilities
■ ■ ■ The following examples again ask the learners to distinguish the meaning of chunks – but with slightly different grammatical priming: the meaning is affected by the grammatical change ('deixis') rather than word order.

| | |
|---|---|
| a blue one and a white one | a blue and white one |
| Have you seen a dog? | Have you seen the dog? |
| Have you got an ashtray? | Have you got that ashtray? |
| on the way | in the way |
| make some toast | make a toast |

The examples below ask the learners to distinguish meaning where it is primed by a change in word order, part of speech and addition of an article.

| | | | |
|---|---|---|---|
| role play | play a role | cow herd | herd a cow |
| game plan | plan a game | bike wheel | wheel a bike |
| car park | park a car | bike ride | ride a bike |

**Connects to**
*Opinion versus data* (87) ▪ *Questions, queries and quibbles* (97)

## Restricted access

Chunks have restrictions in the way they are used. Sometimes these are grammatical – *to my mind* is fine, but not *to his mind*. Sometimes they are contextual: a person can be as *warm as toast* but not the weather. Learners need to develop a feel for these limitations through exposure.

Level ⬜ ■ ■   Duration ● ● ◡

### Preparation
Collect and make copies of sample sentences by your learners which contain misuses of chunks (see the sample text below). You also need sets of various dictionaries and, if possible, internet access.

### Procedure
- Give out the copies of the misused sentences you have collected, or use the sample text below:
  *To his mind it is important.
  *Entertainment is a lion's share in his life.
  *It's warm as toast outside.
  *The president is the cat's whiskers in the US.
  *I agree with you up to a certain extent.
  *I am tired in my book.

- Explain that all the sentences are interesting examples of learners trying to use chunks they have learned, but not fully absorbed – they are interesting errors that say a lot about the limitations of chunks.

- Ask the learners to get into pairs or threes and, using dictionaries and/or internet access, to spot the mistake in each sentence and correct it.

- Discuss their answers. (A useful distinction to make is whether the error is due to the *context* in which it is used or a *grammatical* restriction.)

- Start an ongoing project of looking for or spotting misuse of chunks.

### Possibilities
Collect a set of learners' attempts to use fixed expressions by translating them literally from L1. For example, a Polish learner might translate a Polish idiom and say '*like peas against the wall*' meaning '*like water off a duck's back*', '*like an elephant in the china shop*' for '*like a bull in a china shop*' or '*as deaf as a tree trunk*' for '*as deaf as a post*'.
- Collect some that the learners have used which are *correct*.
- Mix up the correct and incorrect ones and give out the list, saying that they have been used by someone in the class.
- Ask them to work out: Which are right? Which are wrong?

**Connects to**
*Colourful clichés* (67) ▪ *Questions, queries and quibbles* (97)

## Grammar in chunks

Some grammar structures are best taught as chunks. In this activity, the learners approach a grammar structure through chunks associated with it. There is also an underlying emotion behind some grammar structures which is important for understanding.

Level ⬜ ■ ■   Duration ● ● ◡

### Procedure
- Put the learners into pairs and give an example or two of a spoken passive:
  *get lost    get tired    get annoyed*

- Ask them to come up with exactly ten examples of their own. They must follow the structure, so make it clear that you want 'get + past participle' – not just any chunk beginning with 'get'.

- When most of the learners have got ten examples, tell them they have to do a little maths:
  □ What percentage have a negative meaning?
  □ Which are neutral?
  □ Which are positive?

- When they have done the maths, ask them to give their percentages.

- Hold a brief discussion. Results and interpretations vary but, in our experience, the learners come up with many more negative examples than positive ones.

- Finally, ask the learners to translate a few examples into written English. For example:
  *get burgled* → more formal written English → *my house was burgled*

### Possibilities
Some other structures have a negative connotation and can be used in this activity:
□ '*She tends to be a bit* + adjective' suggests a negative adjective.
□ '*Cause*' is usually negative: '*cause accidents*', '*cause problems*', etc.

Some structures are positive in connotation:
□ '*Provide*', as in '*provide care*' or '*provide a solution*', is an example of a structure which is more often primed in a positive way.

**Connects to**
*Get this!* (37) ▪ *Environment / Grammar* (98)

# Real-life responses

In real life, we rarely respond to a question with the same grammatical form as the original utterance – it is the relationship to the speaker (and shared knowledge) that gives meaning to the response. Here, the learners get a taste of 'authenticity' and a way of establishing their own criteria for what is possible.

Level  Duration ● ◡ ◡

10 minutes in the first lesson, a couple of minutes outside class, 20 minutes in another lesson

## Lesson One

- Introduce the phrase *'It's not my day today'*. Check that the learners know what it means and when it is used.

- Ask what a strictly 'correct' grammatical response would be – perhaps: *'Nor is it mine'* or *'It's not mine either'*.

- Ask each learner, for homework, to try the phrase *'It's not my day today'* as an opening gambit on a chosen native speaker (see the Possibilities below if all your class don't have access to a native speaker).

- Brainstorm the names of native speakers the learners have access to: either in their environment, or native speakers they contact on Skype or Twitter. Get them to focus on one person each, so that they don't all pick on the same one.
  - They need to use their gambit in open conversation and not ask the native speaker what they would say.
  - They should remember the response and note it down for the future lesson.

- Set a time limit for the learners to ask their chosen speaker.

## Lesson Two

- Pool all the responses. Some of our classes came back with the contents of the box opposite.

- The responses in the utterances are unlikely to be a 'grammatical' match to the original utterance – this is worth opening up to a brief discussion with the learners.

## Possibilities

You can ask the class to try out the phrases on non-native speakers (for example learners from a higher class in the school). Compare *their* responses with the native-speakers'.

As an awareness-raising activity, the learners can do the 'research' part of the activity in their mother tongue – German learners could ask the question *'Wie gehts?'* and record the answers. In class, they compare their findings.

---

**'It's not my day today'**

- *Oh … and why?*
- *… (laughs) …*
- *I think it's nobody's day today, isn't it. Go and have a lie down.*
- *Oh dear …*
- *Make it your day.*
- *Not being able to be creative* (laughs).
- *Hangover?*
- *Would you like to talk about it?*
- *Me neither. Everything I've done's gone wrong.*
- *Pardon? … Have some of these* (offers aspirin).
- *Oh you don't, do you? Did you manage it?*
- *Is everything alright? Everyone seems to be having a bad day today.*
- *I'll tell you what to do … you should go to the bookshop.*

Of course, you can use any phrase of your choice:
- *'It's going to be one of those days'* is another good one.
- *'How's life?'* or *'What's new?'* are suitable for lower-level classes. We got the following responses:

**'What's new?'**

- *Not much, what's up with you lot? Did you have a really late night or something?*
- *Ha, ha, ha, HA … I got an apology from the nurses.*
- *Nothing really, what's new with yourself?*
- *Pussycat … nothing much.*
- *Nothing.*
- *Not much. Except I'm 36 today.*
- *Nothing, my eye's getting better.*
- *… (sings) …*
- *Nothing. But there will be shortly. What are you doing today?*
- *Pardon … oh, you're doing your homework.*

---

**Connects to**
*Answers to questions* (29)

## Gossip, not communication

Expressing oneself and 'gossiping' is the main purpose of speaking. Learners really need to 'listen to each other' – here we highlight *back-channelling* and *response tokens* – improving group empathy and improving self esteem. It works better if they already know each other well.

Level ■ ■ ■    Duration ● ● ◡

### Preparation
It is useful if you have already done *Top 20 words* (page 86) and to have ready copies of the list of words.

### Procedure
- Write on the board:
    yeah    mm … mm    I know    you know
- Recap how these expressions might be used to 'lubricate' a conversation between two 'gossipers'.
- The learners form threes, find somewhere comfortable to sit and comment on the colour of each other's eyes (this is to form the group). Give them a moment for this.
- Ask them to choose roles – one listener, two speakers.
    □ The 'listener' sits with their *back* to the 'speakers'.
    □ The speakers have one minute to gossip about the listener.
- Time the minute, and stop them. (At this point, the listeners will normally want to comment on what was said about them – ask them to refrain from this.)
- Repeat the activity with the other two learners taking turns to be gossiped about.
- End with a discussion: Did the *mms* and *yeahs* help the flow of the conversation? Can this be applied to real life?
- Give out the Top 20 and ask the learners to notice the positions of *yeah*, *mm* and *(I/you) know*. Together, they represent approximately 5% of the English language!

### Possibilities
You might want to instruct your learners to say only positive things – we found this to be unnecessary (especially if you explain that they will *all* be gossiped about). Gossip is a rather negative word but, in fact, most gossip is positive. (In *Grooming, Gossip and the Origins of Language*, Robin Dunbar shows that about 65% of language is for gossip – with roughly equal amounts for men and women.)

This type of activity (learnt from Bonnie Tsai) can also be helpful in preparing the 'conversation' part of any exam.

**Connects to**
*Top 20 words* (86) ▪ *Conversation countdown* (58)

## Fixed expression rituals

This activity shows that fixed expressions are used more often than not to 'bond' or express a shared feeling.

Level ◻ ■ ■    Duration ● ◡ ◡

### Procedure
- Write the following on the board:
    *It's a funny old world.*
    *Who would have thought it?*
    *There's nowt so queer as folk.*
    *Well, well, well.*
- Check the learners understand the chunks, and ask them to suggest a situation using all four of the above.
- The logical answer is that it would be a 'ritual pause', probably in a pub – if the drinks and the gossip have finished. In a social situation, there is often a ritual repetition of 'nonsense' idioms/fixed expressions, grouped for pragmatic effect. Explain that what is indicated here is that it's time to decide whether to have another round of drinks – or else break up the group and continue another day.
- It may be useful to compare with what happens in the learners' home culture.

### Possibilities
◻ ■ ■ Sketch a diagram on the board of three people at a restaurant table (two colleagues and a boss) and a waiter. (We learnt this activity from Mike McCarthy.)

Write the following three stems on the board:
*I'll …*    *I'm going to have …*    *I'd like …*

Explain the situation: the boss has invited two workers who are colleagues to lunch. In British culture, the boss would be expected to pay – check if this is the same in the culture of the learners.

Now set the task: *Who would say what to whom?*

Give the learners a couple of minutes and then check, explaining that – according to corpus research – the answer is precise:
□ The boss would say *'I'm going to have …'* to the two colleagues.
□ They would say *'I'd like to have …'* to the boss.
□ The colleagues would say *'I'm going to have …'* to each other.
□ All three would normally say *'I'll have …'* to the waiter.

Again, open up to a general discussion.

**Connects to**
*Colourful clichés* (67) ▪ *Grammar in chunks* (63)

## What was the question?

This activity encourages learners to realise that expressing yourself successfully is often dependent on shared knowledge, not just on command of the language.

Level ⬜ ■ ■     Duration ● ● ◡

### Preparation
In the staffroom, or among other English-speaking people you know, ask the same question (see below). Write down the answers. Select and arrange a maximum of seven answers – from the most enigmatic to the relatively obvious.

### Procedure
- Tell the learners that they are going to play a game and to get into teams of four or five.
- The aim is to guess the original question from the seven authentic replies that you give. Write the first *reply* to the question on the board. For example: *Unfortunately.*
- The learners guess the question, eg: *Do you smoke?*
- Write on the board another *reply* to your question, eg:
    *Unfortunately.*
    *Yes, 20 years ago.*
- They have to find the question that both replies answer, eg: *Did you get married?*
- Carry on until you have written all the answers on the board (see the sample text below) or until one group guesses the original question:
    *Unfortunately.*
    *Yes, 20 years ago.*
    *I am too embarrassed to say.*
    *That's what they tell me.*
    *Let's have a look!*
    *I take after him, don't I?*

    The question: Is that your father in the photo?

### Possibilities
This activity can be used to introduce an element of culture. Ask the same question to a number of native speakers, or non-natives with a high command of English, and collect the answers. However, as you can see from the examples below, sometimes the replies may not be what you expect:

*I try not to. / It's O.K. / They are finished./ Very expensive! A bunch of idiots!/ Inbred collection of misfits. / They get on my nerves, except for the Queen, maybe as she's more discreet.*

The question: What do you think about the Royal Family?

**Connects to**
Answers to questions (29) ▪ Real-life responses (64)

## Old versus young

This activity aims to raise awareness of using 'colourful' fixed expressions. Learners at more advanced levels tend to use those expressions they know *indiscriminately*. Since the use of a lot of fixed expressions is age- and gender-related, they are relatively rare in open speech.

Level ⬜ ■ ■     Duration ● ◡ ◡

### Preparation
Make a selection of fixed expressions/clichés, choosing a mix of old-fashioned ones and fairly new ones.

### Procedure
- Give out the examples you have prepared (see the sample text below) and check understanding. For example:
    *I don't believe it.*
    *Oh my god.*
    *Burst a blood vessel.*
    *It's so not true.*
    *Keep right on to the end of the road.*
    *Going great guns.*
    *They is mad, innit?*
    *Stuff happens.*
    *Christmas comes but once a year.*
    *No way.*
    *Beyond the pale.*
- Ask the learners to divide the fixed expressions into four groups:
    ☐ Said by older people.
    ☐ Said by young people.
    ☐ Said by both.
    ☐ Not sure.
- Give the groups enough time, and then check with the whole class.
- Discuss. Of course, a lot of your learners will no doubt have opted for the 'Not sure' answer – but, in any case, much interesting discussion should be generated.

### Possibilities
Collect a list of young persons' expressions/clichés. Ask the learners to divide them into gender-specific groups: *Oh my god*, for example, tends to be said by girls rather than boys. (Advanced learners often have a lot of passive knowledge based on their viewing habits of TV series like *Friends*, etc.)

**Connects to**
Fixed expression rituals (65) ▪ Colourful clichés (67)

# Colourful clichés

At higher levels, learners tend to *over-use* fixed expressions. This activity aims to encourage them to notice how colourful idioms are clichéd and not used 'straight': they are usually 'twisted' and used in a 'knowing way'.

Level    Duration

## Preparation
You will need copies of worksheets (see the sample texts opposite).

## Procedure
- Give out copies of Worksheet 1 opposite.
  - Check that the learners know the meaning of the fixed expressions.
  - Give them time to work on the questions.
- After discussion of the questions on the worksheet, give out Worksheet 2.
- Discuss the idea of 'twisted clichés' with the learners.

## Possibilities
Either you or the learners can collect examples of twisted clichés for future lessons.

You can ask your learners what 'normal' clichés they know in English – or you give them a list:
- *Too many cooks spoil the broth.*
- *Many hands make light work.*
- *All work and no play makes Jack a dull boy.*

You then ask them to come up with some twisted clichés.

The first example we found on the Web when we consulted 'twisted clichés' was:
*An apple a day keeps the doctor away.*
↓
*An apple a day still can't beat pizza.*

Using the list you have compiled, you can get the learners to 'twist' them:
*Too many cooks …*
*Many hands …*
*All work and no play …*

The learners can think of more for the next lesson.

### Worksheet 1

**Fixed expressions, idioms or clichés?**
Comment on the following fixed expressions (idioms).
1. A bird in the hand is worth two in the bush.
2. It's not rocket science/brain surgery.
3. Thinking outside the box.
4. I could have curled up and died.
5. An elephant in the room.
6. Shut the gate after the horse has bolted.
7. A pain in the backside.

Would you use these?
How often? In spoken or written English?

Which term do you prefer:
'Fixed expression' or 'idiom' or 'cliché'?

Does the term 'twisted cliché' mean anything to you?

### Worksheet 2

Comment on the following. They are all extracts from the British media.
1. He's throwing away a bird in the hand for two in a bush which hasn't even been planted.
2. It's not rocket surgery.
3. Make sure you know the box before you go out of it.
4. Curl up and dry (name of a hairdressing shop).
5. Only because you managed to trap an elephant and force it rampaging into the room.
6. The words that spring to mind are *horse*, *gate* and *bolted*.
7. A pain in the proverbial.

The examples 6 and 7 above are a good way of twisting clichés:
The **stems** are:
*The words that spring to mind are …*
*… in the proverbial.*
You just have to slot in a cliché.

**Connects to**
*Restricted access* (63) • *Twisted chunks* (75)

## From culture to culture

Politeness is often seen as smiling nicely and saying please and thank you a lot. This activity focuses on the concept of face-saving and politeness, which varies greatly from culture to culture although it is universal. It is worth making reference to the learners' own culture when setting the scene.

Level    Duration ● ● ○

### Preparation
Prepare copies for each learner (see the set of expressions below). You will also need good corpus-based dictionaries.

### Procedure
- Ask the learners to look up the word 'face' (in the sense of 'respect') in a good dictionary. Write the chunks they find on the board. For example:

| | | |
|---|---|---|
| save face | lose face | don't get facey with me |
| have egg on your face | | face-saving gesture |
| never show your face again | | loss of face |
| put on a brave face | | face-saving exercise |

- Set the following scene:
  You are walking along the corridor (a narrow corridor). Two colleagues (not your best friends but people you like working with) are having a conversation.
  □ Do you join in the conversation?
  □ Do they want you to join in?
  □ If you walk past without saying anything, will they think you are rude?
  □ If they don't say hello to you, will you feel offended?

- Ask the learners to spend a moment visualising the situation.

- Tell them that the kind of decision they make and the language they use can involve 'a loss of face'. Say that the situation outlined above happens on a daily, if not hourly, basis to most of us.

- Give out, or write on the board, the samples (these are at intermediate level) below:

| | |
|---|---|
| Don't let me disturb you. | Hold on a moment! |
| Come on. | We were just talking about … |
| Don't go away. | Hope to catch you later. |
| Come and join us. | Must rush. |
| Carry on. | Got a moment? |

- Ask the learners to divide the utterances into two categories:
  □ Positive politeness – *trying to 'include'*
  □ Negative politeness – *trying not to invade personal space or interrupt*

- They should also say who is most likely to say each utterance:
  □ The two already having a conversation?
  □ The person walking along the corridor?

- Discuss their answers and any additional items of language they come up which are suitable for the situation. Note that some of the utterances above could be used for both positive *and* negative politeness, eg *We were just talking about … .*

### Possibilities
■ ■ You can write a different set of chunks for more advanced learners:

*overbearing     … totally insensitive     … makes me cringe
keeps a low profile     puts you at ease
a bit pushy     a bit abrupt     a complete creep
a bit standoffish     over-familiar*

Discuss the meanings. Ask the learners to suppose that the interaction in the activity above goes badly wrong and is seen as typical of that person:
□ Which of the chunks suggest being *too* negatively polite?
□ Which suggest being *too* positively polite?

---

**Connects to**
*Top 100 collocations* (87) • *Conversational manoeuvres* (45)

# Chapter Four
## In authentic contexts

Authentic English is potentially difficult – but the earlier the learners are exposed to it, the more successful they will be. We can offer them a type of blended learning, merging what they learn in class with what they encounter in their environment. Blurring this distinction can raise awareness of genre and develop inner criteria for what is likely international English – and what is 'lost in translation'.

### The world we live in

It is difficult to imagine any of our learners walking along a street, going into a kitchen or bathroom or browsing the media anywhere in the world – and not encountering English chunks. English is the international language of choice and English chunks are used in most languages, just as English has borrowed from many other languages. Learners are exposed to authentic text as part of their everyday life – and the activities here aim to make use of this.

The first activities ask the learners to notice and collect the English that surrounds them – on packets, ephemera, on their mobiles. Even a bus journey can become an independent learning experience!

### The words we live with

These activities involve working with different types of authentic text: newspapers, literature, songs, film. The Web has made these easier for us to find – and easier for the learners to find, too. Where we have chosen examples of songs and literature, we have tried to find text which mirrors the features of natural spoken English and is not too literary in style.

Songs and films are an area where learners can show what they know, and they can collect their own examples – many being found in the original language, with subtitles or translations. The chapter ends with 'live' listening activities – the learners compare chunks in English with chunks in their own language. Using their language as a resource is a neglected area in English Language Teaching.

## Cut it out!

Many packages in the learners' world have chunks in English. Bringing examples to class encourages the learners to notice how much English there is in their everyday environment.

**15 minutes the first lesson,
10 minutes in a subsequent lesson**

### Preparation
Bring to class a few English chunks cut out of packaging (or photo the chunks and get printouts). You will also need materials to stick the cut-outs on the wall or on the board.

### Procedure
- Get all the learners standing around the notice board or a blank wall space.
- Show your cut-outs, explain what they are and where you got them, and attach them to the wall.
- As homework, ask the learners to bring more to add to the wall display:
  - Tell them that they should not be single words but chunks.
  - Tell them that the kitchen or bathroom is a good place to find them.
- In a subsequent lesson, add the contributions to the wall (and re-set the homework) – and discuss them.

### Possibilities
■ ■ ■ You can prepare slips of paper and pin *translations* alongside each chunk. The translation will show, in context, that there is chunking in the learners' L1 as well – but often no exact equivalent.

■ ■ ■ An element of competition often makes this activity go better, especially with younger learners. The class can be divided into teams competing to collect the most cut-out chunks. If you have a roughly equal number of boys and girls in the class, have a boys' wall and a girls' wall; or get two different classes competing.
You can award extra points for longer chunks:
- two-word chunks, 1 point
- three words, 2
- four words, 4
- five words, 8

This scoring system also encourages the learners to notice where chunks begin and end.

**Connects to**
*'Brain sludge'* (29) • *Song titles (and brackets)* (79)

# Signs and notices

Learners are often unaware of how much they are exposed to English chunks in their native surroundings – it is good to weed through their unconscious knowledge and turn this exposure into a conscious learning process: to notice chunks and their appropriate use.

Level ▪ ▪ ▪   Duration ● ● ◡

## Preparation
Research English chunks in your own town or district and prepare a handout for each learner. (We found a good 40 samples, collected in a medium-sized Polish town during a 45-minute drive.)

## Procedure
- Brainstorm English chunks that the learners see on a daily basis where they live, and write them on the board.
- Discuss if they are appropriate English chunks or not.
  *night shop* – unlikely in an English-speaking country: a non-native chunk
  *Black and White* (pub) – a non-native attempt at Britishness: unlikely
  *passenger airbag* – likely international English
- Give out the handout you have prepared.
- The learners work individually and decide how likely the chunks are in an international context. They then compare their answers with a partner.
- Pool all the findings and discuss.
- Set homework, in which the learners research chunks themselves, for further discussion in future lessons.

## Possibilities
The activity can become an ongoing project, with the findings printed out and displayed on the wall – the learners take photos of the chunks with their mobile phone cameras.

You can hold a competition by dividing the class into small teams and allocating a place in town to each group – airport, shopping mall, etc. The teams collect the chunks and present them in class, keeping the place a secret while the others guess what place it was and say what gave them the clue.

▫ ▫ ▪ You can choose more precise criteria for evaluation – American/British English, trendy/chic, attempts at sophistication, borrowings, translations, language play, etc.

Websites such as *www.engrish.com* are a useful source of 'mangled' chunks.

**Connects to**
*Film titles* (80) ▪ *Going for a song* (91)

# Going shopping

Learners are often unaware that they are surrounded by chunks and that we don't always write them in full. Receipts and shopping lists offer insights into culture, lifestyle and language. We came up with this idea when trying to remember why we bought WUL – washing-up liquid in 'supermarket speak'.

Level ▪ ▪ ▪   Duration ● ● ◡

## Preparation
Collect of a set of shopping lists and authentic receipts from English supermarkets and copy them for each learner or pair of learners (see the examples below).

## Procedure
- Ask the learners to think of a regular shopping list in their home and to write their list in English. Help with any language problems.
- The learners then compare their lists.
- Give out the copies of the receipts and lists to the learners:
  - They work in pairs or on their own.
  - They compare their shopping lists in English with with what you have given them.
  - They look for items from their own lists in the receipts and lists you have provided.
- Discuss what they have noticed about the way the receipts are worded.

## Possibilities
You can ask the learners to study a particular receipt and do some detective work. They have to decide who the shopper was. For example:

| age | day of the week | season |
| profession | family status | occasion |

You can download from the internet weird shopping lists found by accident: *http://www.foundmagazine.com*. The learners use their imagination and write a story around them.

The learners can design 'receipts of the future' – for 2150!

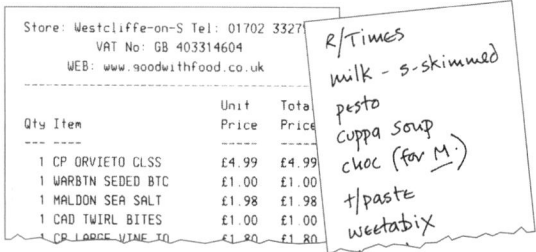

**Connects to**
*Headline collage* (73)

## 'To do' lists

This activity researches the learner corpus around a topic area, pools chunks around one lexical area – and adds new chunks.

Level ☐ ■ ■     Duration ● ● ◡

### Preparation
Prepare cards with situations, as well as some sheets of paper, one per pair or group of learners (see below for examples).

### Procedure
- Ask the learners to write down the things they need to do before a summer holiday.
- Invite suggestions and write them up under **TO DO**.
- Discuss the chunks the learners have come up with, invite comments and, if necessary, translate them into English.
- Put the learners into pairs or groups and give out the situation cards you have prepared. Ask them to keep the cards secret. For example:

| before Christmas | before doing up a room |
| before giving a party | before a job interview |
| before spring cleaning in the garden | before babysitting a five-year-old niece |

- The learners brainstorm things that need doing on pieces of paper, making sure they don't write the *situation* anywhere on the page.
- Monitor and help with any language problems, then circulate the sheets for others to guess the situation.
- Bring the class together and discuss any chunks they would like to add to the lists.

### Possibilities
The learners can come up with their own situations, instead.

◡ ■ ■ You can prepare a list of more *unlikely* situations – getting ready to catch a criminal, to persuade your partner to spend a weekend with your mother, etc. You can find 'to do' lists on the internet at *http://www.foundmagazine.com*. Most lists don't have a subject written at the top: the learners can guess what the person was getting ready for. The nice thing is that there is no correct answer.

This activity can help to prepare for some exam tasks which involve 'cutting down' full grammatical text to make lists which are mostly lexical chunks.

**Connects to**
Answers to questions (29) • Rapid repairs (62)

## Textspeak

Learners probably already use textspeak in their L1. Here, we aim to familiarise them with trends in writing text chunks in English and researching them on the Web. (UK research has shown that teenagers who are good at textspeak are above average when writing in other genres.)

Level ☐ ■ ■     Duration ● ● ◡

### Preparation
Prepare a handout – with text messages illustrating the features of the genre in the *left-hand column* and the 'translations' in the *right-hand column*, as in the sample below. You can find plenty more examples on the internet. For example at: *http://en.wikipedia.org/wiki/SMS_language*.

### Procedure
- Brainstorm with the learners what they know about texting in English: acronyms, disenvowelling, abbreviation – and anything else they might have noticed.
- Give out your samples, asking the learners to fold the page so they cannot see the key. They have to work out the meanings of the textspeak in the left-hand column.

| U2 | you too |
| 121 | one to one |
| BRB | be right back |
| BTW | by the way |
| CUL | see you later |
| F2F | face to face |
| FYI | for your information |
| TIA | thanks in advance |
| WTG | way to go |
| TTFN | ta-ta for now |
| LOL | laughing out loud |
| HHOK | ha ha only kidding |

- Ask the learners to unfold the handout and check answers.
- Discuss the features of texting genre in the examples.
- In pairs, the learners write messages or exchanges using some of the expressions, then circulate the texts so that other learners can read them.

### Possibilities
The learners all put their mobile numbers into a hat, and then choose one secretly and text that person. This can be done on their mobiles, or using the free text-sending facility of computers if you have computers available.

The learners can look on the Web and bring *their* examples.

**Connects to**
Literature through textspeak (77)

# Advanced txtspk

The genre of textspeak (txtspk) is great fun when used for writing a standard text and, as with the previous activity, raises awareness of acronyms, disenvoweling and abbreviations as types of chunking.

Level ▫▪▪    Duration ●●○

## Preparation
Find examples of whole texts written in textspeak (a useful website is *http://en.wikipedia.org/wiki/SMS_language*) but which are not text messages, or use the sample texts opposite. Prepare separate copies of the texts and the key. If you have internet access in class, it may be useful to call up *http://acronyms.thefreedictionary.com*.

## Procedure
- Elicit the features of texting that the learners already know.
- As a warm-up, give out the sample text in the first box opposite and ask the learners to decipher it.
- When they have finished, check their answers with the key.
- Now divide the class into two groups:
    - One group receives Text A opposite.
    - One group receives Text B.
- In pairs, the learners decipher their text and write it in full English, then they compare their answers within Group A and Group B.
- Then an A-pair and a B-pair exchange their full texts and try to re-write them in textspeak.
- They compare their versions with the original version.
- Finally, bring the class together and discuss.

## Possibilities
As homework, you can ask the learners to find similar texts in textspeak – if they search on Google, they will find new texts themselves.

As in the previous activity, all the learners put their mobile numbers into a hat and then choose one secretly and mail that person. This can be done on the learners' mobiles or using the text-sending facility of computers if you have a computer lab available.

### Sample text
i fot ur rticl wz rly gd. no1 evr speekz up 4 txtng bt i fink itz bril coz itz so much fastr nd eazier 2 read az well. fanx!

### Key
I thought your article was really good. No one ever speaks up for texting but I think it's brilliant because it's so much faster and easier to read as well. Thanks.

### Text A
My smmr hols wr CWOT. B4, we usd 2go2 NY 2C my bro, his GF & thr 3 :- kds
Bt my Ps wr so {:-/ BC o 9/11 tht they dcdd 2 stay in SCO & spnd 2wks up N.
Up N, WUCIWUG -- 0. I ws vvv brd in MON. 0 bt baas & ^^^^^.

### Text B
AAR8, my Ps wr :-) -- they sd ICBW, & tht they wr ha-p 4 the pc&qt...IDTS!! I wntd 2 go hm ASAP, 2C my M8s again.<
2day, I cam bk 2 skool. I feel v :-) BC I hv dn all my hm wrk. Now its BAU...

### Key to Text A
My summer holidays were a complete waste of time. Before, we used to go to New York to see my brother, his girlfriend and their three screaming kids face to face. But my parents were so worried because of September 11th that they decided to stay in Scotland and spend two weeks up North. Up North, what you see is what you get. Nothing. I was very, very, very bored in the middle of nowhere. Nothing but sheep and mountains.

### Key to Text B
At any rate my parents were happy. They said it could be worse and that they were happy for the peace and quiet. I don't think so! I wanted to go home as soon as possible to see my mates again. Today I came back to school. I feel very happy because I have done all my homework. Now it is business as usual.

**Connects to**
*Textspeak* (71) ▪ *Literature through textspeak* (77)

## Headline collage

Newspaper headlines, by their nature, catch the eye, so when the learners leave the classroom they will hopefully continue noticing that chunks are everywhere – the chunks they are becoming accustomed to noticing in class.

Level ▫■■   Duration ●●○

### Preparation
Prepare a pile of English newspapers and/or magazines – they need not be very recent ones, just ones you don't mind being cut up. Prepare scissors, glue and an A3 sheet of blank paper for each pair or group of learners.

### Procedure
- Working with their partners, ask the learners to look through the newspapers and magazines, focusing on the headlines.
- When they come across an interesting chunk in a headline, they cut it out and paste it onto their blank sheet of paper.
- Offer your help to pairs who have doubts as to whether the chunk they have selected is really a chunk.
- When the collages are ready, or the time you have allocated for this activity is up, exhibit them.
- The learners mingle, look at the display and compare the results of their research.
- Finally, discuss what chunks they have learned.

### Possibilities
If you don't want the learners to ruin the newspapers, they can copy the headlines, using different writing styles, or photocopy the ones with the chunks they want to use for their collage. The advantage here is that more than one group will be able to select the same headline.

If you have the facilities, you can do an internet version of the activity. Make sure each group of learners has access to the internet and that the final product of their work can be printed out. Give the learners a handout with lists of newspaper sites they can visit to select the chunks and copy and paste them into a separate file. Finally, print the work out – and exhibit.

**Connects to**
*Cut it out!* (69) ▪ *Twisted chunks* (75)

## Old words, new partnerships

This activity is a confidence booster, especially at lower levels, as it shows the learners that the few words they know are of great importance. Also, it is an important awareness-raising activity, demonstrating that 'a little is a lot' and encouraging the learners to expand the use of already-known lexis into different chunks.

Level ■■■   Duration ●○○

### Preparation
Select a text (ideally, an advert with text in different fonts and sizes and with a picture – to make it learner-friendly). Count how many words the text consists of and make a copy for all the learners, who also need highlighters or coloured pens.

### Procedure
- Give out your prepared texts and ask the learners, working alone, to highlight all the words they know.
- If the same word appears a few times, they highlight it *every time* they come across it. Tell them not to worry about anything else.
  - They count the words they have highlighted.
  - They calculate the percentage that the words they know constitute in the text. (Most learners have a calculator on their mobiles, and so it is easy to work out the percentages.)
  - They compare their results with their neighbours.
- Write the following information on the board (the figures were taken at an Oxford University Press dictionary presentation), using L1 for lower levels if necessary:

> The first 1000 words constitute:
>     74.1% of language
> The second 1000 constitute:
>     7.2% (74.1% + 7.2% = 81.3% )
> The third 1000:
>     3.9% (81.3% + 3.9% = 85.2%)
> The fourth 1000:
>     2.4% (85.2% + 2.4% = 87.6%)
> The fifth 1000:
>     1.8% (87.6% + 1.8% = 89.4%)

- Ask the learners to notice how many times they have underlined the same word.
- Discuss the results, especially in what *different* contexts the *same word* appeared.
- Explain that they not only need to learn *new words* but also new *partnerships* made up of 'old' words.

**Connects to**
*Pass the chunk* (34) ▪ *Top 20 words* (86)

## Chunks in the news

This activity helps the learners to pool lexical items around a theme and look for and recognise chunks in a new text, emphasising the importance of *expressions* rather than *single words* – and of memorising whole chunks.

Level ⌐ ■ ■   Duration ● ● ◡

### Preparation
Prepare a 'plain' copy of a news article you have selected, another copy with some chunks underlined, and a list of chunks that have the *same meaning* as the chunks underlined. This list of paraphrased chunks should be jumbled up so they are not in the same order as the originals in the text. You will need a set for each learner.

### Procedure
- Give out the plain copy of the article and ask the learners to read the text and indicate useful chunks they spot.
- Remind them that chunks will normally be from one word to up to seven words.
- Discuss their individual choices with the whole class.
- Give out the second version of the text, the one with the chunks underlined by you, and ask the learners to compare.
- Discuss *their* choices and *your* choices.
- In pairs, ask the learners how they would *paraphrase* the meanings of the underlined chunks.
- Give out *your* prepared list of equivalent chunks, and ask the learners to match them with the equivalent chunks in the text.
- The learners put the texts away and you read the article:
  - They *stand up* when they hear the chunks they were working on.
  - They *sit down* when the chunks end.

### Possibilities
In the reading aloud stage, instead of making the learners stand up when they hear a familiar chunk, you can pause *before* the chunks, and the learners say the chunk that is about to come in the text.

If you use online texts, this also points the learners towards available resources on the internet, and may encourage them to take the initiative and become more autonomous learners.

**Connects to**
*Listening for chunks* (33) ▪ *Reading for chunks* (33)

## Speculative summaries

This activity introduces the idea of lifting chunks from a text, creating a pool of chunks around a theme chosen by the learners, and then using these chunks in an active way.

Level ⌐ ■ ■   Duration ● ● ●

### Preparation
You need a batch of past newspapers (or internet access in class) for each pair or group of three learners. Do this activity after you have done *Chunks in the news*.

### Procedure
- Remind the learners of *Chunks in the news*.
- Spread out the newspapers, pair or group the learners and ask them to chose a topic – possibly one in which they feel weak or that might come up in an exam.
- Give the learners a few minutes to scan the newspapers. They have to find an article of some 800 words on the subject they have chosen.
- They then select 15 chunks of various lengths, related to the subject they have chosen. You monitor and help.
  - They choose representative chunks from the whole article.
  - They write their chunks on a piece of paper.
  - They hand the lists to another pair.
- The learners have to speculate what the original article was about, as precisely as possible, and then write a 'summary' of the article *they haven't yet seen*, using the chunks they have been given.
- Give the learners the original article to compare the two versions.

### Possibilities
⌐ ■ ■ You can select your own chunks from a newspaper article or advert. The chunks must be puzzling (see the sample below). The learners have to guess what the main subject of the text is:

*heavy duty*
*reusable*
*one size fits both men and women*
*a must for emergency car repair*
*great for sporting events*

Answer: emergency raincoat

When the learners have got the idea from you, they can research and create similar puzzles for each other.

**Connects to**
*Chunks in the news* (74)

# Twisted chunks

Twisting fixed chunks (clichés) is a cultural phenomenon, particularly in newspaper headlines. Advanced learners can use their general knowledge and the internet search engines to enjoy the wordplay – while learning about fixed and 'twisted' chunks.

Level ⬜ ⬜ ■   Duration ● ● ○

## Preparation
Prepare a handout with a selection of headlines which contain 'twisted' chunks (or use the sample text below). To round off the activity, internet research facilities are useful – if available.

## Procedure
- Explain to the learners that, very often, newspaper headlines contain fixed chunks and clichés. However, often they are 'twisted' and played with.
- Give the following example of a twisted cliché: *Raining kittens and puppies*
- Explain or discuss how *Raining cats and dogs* becomes *Raining kittens and puppies* (for 'light rain').
- Refer the learners to their L1. Probably it's the same: clichés are not used so much in open speech, but they are there as cultural concepts to play with.
- Put the learners into pairs and give out your text (see the box below).
    - They have to decide how the chunks in the headline have or could have been twisted or have acquired a double meaning.
    - They can try to google the chunks if the facility is available.

> 1 There's madness in the method
> 2 Still following the leader
> 3 The bore of the worlds
> 4 Kabul: two tales of one city
>
> **Key**
> 1 'Though this be madness, yet there is method in't.' – quote from Shakespeare's *Hamlet*
> 2 *Following the Leader* – title of theme song from Disney cartoon based on J M Barrie's *Peter Pan*
> 3 *The War of the Worlds* – title of an H G Wells' novel
> 4 *A Tale of Two Cities* – title of a C Dickens' novel

## Possibilities
⬜ ■ ■ You can look for some articles that have got a twisted chunk in the headlines. Copy the titles and jumble them up. Lift a few chunks from the articles, as in the sample below. In pairs, the learners try to match the set of chunks to the headline. Discuss how the chunk was 'twisted' and how it acquired a new meaning.

> A  Making a dog's dinner of a pet food campaign (2011)
> B  Message in a big bottle (2011)
> C  Big Brother isn't watching you (2011)
> D  Classic without a twist (2005)

> 1  review of Polanski's film 'Oliver Twist', novel by Dickens, not original enough, won't have audiences asking for more, an impersonal experience

> 2  model of Nelson's flagship, public appeal, launched a campaign, text message donations, keeping it in the public domain, keep it at Greenwich

> 3  complete mess, ignoring all expert advice, to promote a pet food, pitching a product, overweight cat market, ignoring efforts, packaging and marketing

> 4  novel by George Orwell, The Big Brother nightmare, vision of a society, cameras and computers spy on every person's movements, the UK riots, reality TV

From: *The Guardian* – the year is next to the headline.

⬜ ⬜ ■ You explain how the sample text was produced, and the learners prepare similar sets: headlines and sets of key chunks lifted from the articles. The headlines and chunks circulate from pair to pair and the learners match the title with the chunks.

---

**Connects to**
*Colourful clichés* (67) ▪ *Restricted access* (63)

## Howzaboutit?

Elision often takes place when pronouncing chunks. Learners should be made aware that a chunk, a phrase or a sentence is often *pronounced* like one word. We collected the samples here from newspapers and adverts, but modern novels are also a good source.

Level ■ ■ ■    Duration ● ● ◡

### Preparation
Copy a list of phrases and sentences where the writer has made two or more words into a single word to emphasise the pronunciation in spoken English.

### Procedure
- Say, at speed, the phrases *Good night*, *Good bye*, *Have a good day* and *Never mind*, and ask the learners how many words they really hear.
- Ask them to write down what they really hear in alternative spelling (or 'text message' speak), for example: *gdnite*, *gdby*, etc.
- Give out the samples below and ask the learners to write the full form:

| | |
|---|---|
| a wannabe | Whaddayaknow? |
| whodunit | Whassematter? |
| kinda one-sided | Yerallright. |
| awright | Whadjergonnado? |
| | Whossat? |
| Howzit going? | Howssat? |
| D'jew think 'e's got it? | Omigod! |
| C'mon love | Fugheddaboutit. |
| Lemme have it! | Warraboutit? |
| You're outta here? | |
| Make a career outta that | |

- Discuss the answers.
- In pairs, the learners work on the exact pronunciation of the chunks, trying to make them sound like one word.

### Possibilities
You can start an ongoing project, asking the learners to find similar examples from their own reading.

## Chunks in novels

Lexical density is a feature of literature, too, where utterances and chunks are used rather than full sentences. This activity is a good way of making the learners aware of the chunks used more in spoken rather than written English. Scan reading and reading aloud with appropriate intonation are also practised.

Level ■ ■ ■    Duration ● ● ●

### Preparation
Select a pile of modern novels in their original versions, not abridged. Look through the books you have prepared, to make sure they contain some dialogues with chunks rather than sentences.

### Procedure
- Put the learners into pairs.
- Tell them to look through the books for dialogues in chunks (not just full sentences). Remind them that as long as they roughly understand the dialogue, the rest doesn't matter.
- When the learners have found their dialogues, ask them to rehearse them for a performance.
- The pairs act out their dialogues in front of the class, paying great attention to intonation.
- As the class listen to the dialogue, they have to figure out what is happening.
- Discuss with the whole class – for example:
  - Does it feel like spoken English?
  - How did the chunks help them with intonation?

### Possibilities
For this activity, suggested by Penny Shefton, you can use plays and even poems, instead of using novels – select poems and plays which have naturalistic English dialogues.
For example:
*After Liverpool* – James Saunders
*The Shape of Things* – Neil LaBute

---

**Connects to**
*Literature through textspeak* (77) ▪ *Conversation countdown* (58)

**Connects to**
*Recycling a dialogue* (45) ▪ *7-1 dialogues* (57)

# Literature through textspeak

The learners look at 'textspeak' versions of classic literature to raise their awareness of different registers.

Level    Duration

## Preparation
Prepare handouts of the sample texts opposite. The learners should previously have done *Textspeak* (page 71).

## Procedure
- In small groups, the learners brainstorm English novels or plays they know.
- Each group has to decide on just one and write down in a few sentences a summary of the novel or play.
- Divide the class into three groups. Each receives a summary of a famous piece of English literature in textspeak (see the three samples opposite – our thanks to Penny Shefton for her help) and has to decipher the texts.
- When they have finished, give out the full versions of the texts to compare.
- Regroup the learners – to share their three texts.
- Now bring them back into the groups they were working in at the beginning of the lesson.
- The groups transform their own short summaries into textspeak and then circulate the texts for the others to decipher.

## Possibilities
You can find more texts – for *Romeo and Juliet*, *Pride and Prejudice* and *Bleak House* – in the following article:
'If you don't want to know how Bleak House ends, look away now' by Martin Wainwright, *The Guardian*, Thursday 17 November 2005:
http://www.guardian.co.uk/technology/2005/nov/17/news.mobilephones

You can prepare your own texts with the help of a two-way translation tool – see Plain English to Lingo:
http://www.lingo2word.com/translate.php
The learners can also use this, and other online tools, when writing their own texts or decoding the texts they receive from the other groups.

You can point out that monks making copies of the Magna Carta and other documents in the 13th century omitted vowels and punctuation and made up abbreviations to save on parchment space. An early form of textspeak – or, rather, 'parchmentspeak'!

---

**Gone with the wind**
Scarlett dautA of a mn wh hs a plntatn n Georgia. Shes Nluv w Ashly bt he luvs Melanie. ThN Scrlet mts Rhett, bit of a blck sheep/guy w reputation. ThN Civil War bgins. ppl fyt, suffA, luv, wed, >dosh or di. evntully Scrlet weds Rhett thgs don't wk ot.

**Othello**
Othello isa general hu hs an ambitious pal Iago. wen hes nt promoD he gets vry jLs. So he strts an }-) plot agenst Othello. Othello luvs Desdemona bt hes vry suspicious n jLs. coz of mnE plots Othello kills hs innocent yF, n thN kills himself

**Tom Sawyer**
Tom Sawyer livs w Aunt Polly & hs bro in Mississippi rivA twn. Hes Nluv w Becky/ hs bst frd Huck. Hes a nauty bt charmin boy. Bst moments of bk involv paintn a fence, answerin on d bble, getN 404 n findin a treasure.

**Gone with the wind**
Scarlett is the daughter of a man who owns a plantation in Georgia. She is in love with Ashley but he loves Melanie. Then Scarlett meets Rhett who has quite a reputation. Then the Civil War begins. People fight, suffer, love, marry, lose money or die. Eventually Scarlett marries Rhett but things don't work out.

**Othello**
Othello is a general who has an ambitious friend, Iago. When he is not promoted, he gets very jealous. So he starts an evil plot against Othello. Othello loves Desdemona but he is very suspicious and jealous. Because of many plots, Othello kills his innocent wife, and then kills himself.

**Tom Sawyer**
Tom Sawyer lives with Aunt Polly and his brother in a Mississippi River town. He is in love with Becky and his best friend is called Huck. He is a naughty but charming boy. Best moments of the book involve painting a fence, answering questions on the Bible, getting lost and finding a treasure.

---

**Connects to**
*Advanced txtspk* (72)

# Kiss the sky

The mishearing of chunks in songs (called a 'mondegreen') is a common phenomenon both in our native language and in a foreign language. Awareness of this fact is a confidence booster for the learners, if they see that mishearing is common for native speakers, too.

**Level** ⌐ ■ ■   **Duration** ● ● ◡

## Preparation
Prepare two lists of phrases with potential for mishearing (see the upper-intermediate-level examples below). If you have internet and data projection available, you can connect to *http://www.kissthisguy.com/* or to similar websites of your choice for use in class.

## Procedure
- Dictate the following chunks:
    *I scream for tea*   *Kiss the sky*
- Repeat each one a number of times, saying them fast. Make sure you link up the words well so that the phrases can be interpreted as *'Ice cream for tea'* or *'I scream for tea'*, and *'Kiss the sky'* or *'Kiss this guy'*.
- In pairs, the learners compare what they have written.
- Talk about their alternatives with the whole class and discuss the phenomenon of mishearing – of listening for elision and linking-up.
- Divide the class into two groups and give out your samples – Sample 1 to Group A, Sample 2 to Group B.

> **Sample 1**
> *A girl with colitis goes by*
> *I'd never be your pizza burning*
> *Another one rides the bus*
> *Two chickens in fried rice*

> **Sample 2**
> *Girl with kaleidoscope eyes*
> *I'll never be your beast of burden*
> *Another one bites the dust*
> *Two tickets to paradise*

- Explain that Group A has a list of misheard chunks, Group B the original chunks. The learners can work individually or as two groups:
    - Group A has to predict *what* the original chunks were.
    - Group B has to predict *how* the chunks can be misheard.
- Pair off learners from Groups A and B. They feed across what their predictions were and find out from each other what the handouts said.
- As homework, the learners can research their own examples of mishearing in songs.

## Possibilities
It may be useful to ask the learners for examples of mishearing in their L1.

You can research songs by one artist or even one song. For example:
*http://www.amiright.com/misheard/artist/rollingstones.shtml*

You can play the first stanza/fragment of a song of your choice which lends itself to mishearing and ask the learners to write down what they have heard. In small groups, they compare their notes. Discuss with the whole class their various interpretations.

Collecting 'problem chunks' from listening tasks in the coursebook can become an ongoing project which, with time, will help the learners improve their listening comprehension. Allocate a special place on the wall where you can display these chunks.

**Connects to**
*Mischucking* (49)

## Songs in your head

We all carry in our heads many chunks from texts we are often exposed to. This activity helps us to bring this 'brain sludge' to the surface, talk about it and work on correctness (sometimes these phrases are remembered by learners in very 'approximate' versions).

Level ■ ■ ■   Duration ● ● ○

### Preparation
Prepare an English song that is well known to the learners. Divide each line into halves, making sure that where you divide the lines is the middle of a chunk. An example from the Beatles:

| | |
|---|---|
| Yesterday all my troubles seemed | … so far away |
| It looks as though | … they're here to stay |
| I believe in | … yesterday |
| Why she had to go | … I don't know, she wouldn't say |

### Procedure
- Read out the first half of each line you have prepared – the learners complete it, shouting out the answers.
- Get the learners to think of the names of songs in English that they are crazy about, and for which they know at least some of the lyrics.
- They jot down as many phrases or bits of the lyrics that they can remember.
- In small groups or pairs, learners with similar tastes take it in turns to test each other, reading the first part of a phrase or line and seeing if their partners can continue it.
- Our learners came up with these:

| | |
|---|---|
| I'm a loser baby | … so why don't you kill me? (*Loser* by Beck) |
| I'm just a sucker | … with no self esteem (*Self Esteem* by The Offspring) |

### Possibilities
■ ■ ■ You can prepare a well-known song in the learners' native language, or chunks from various songs. If you do this variation first, the learners will become aware that they know the phenomenon very well and that it is universal – regardless of what language the chunks are in.

⌐ ■ ■ Similar activities can be done with poems, adverts, quotations or book titles. Examples need to come from sources familiar to the learners and liked by them.

**Connects to**
*Listening for chunks* (33)

## Song titles (and brackets)

Song titles, by their very nature, are at the juncture of written and spoken grammar. We have noticed that brackets are often used to show the boundaries that separate one chunk from another. This activity highlights how chunks fit together to form extended utterances.

Level ⌐ ■ ■   Duration ● ● ○

### Preparation
Look through your CDs or MP3 files (or on YouTube/ Myspace) and select a few song titles which have brackets (see the samples below), write them out and make copies. If they are songs by groups well known to the age group of your class, so much the better.

### Procedure
- Write one or two examples on the board, with the song titles still containing their brackets. For example:
  
  *I Don't Want Nobody to Give Me Nothing (Open up the Door I'll Get it Myself)*
  James Brown
  *Inner City Blues (Make Me Want to Holler)*
  Marvin Gaye

- Now dictate your song titles one by one, without saying where the brackets are:
  - Using a flat voice will make this activity more difficult.
  - Alternatively, your intonation can be a helpful clue to make it easier.

- After you dictate each title, the learners have 30 seconds to consult with a neighbour where to insert the brackets.

- Give out the original copies and ask the learners to check if they have put the brackets in the same place. (They may have alternatives to the original which are also likely.)

### Possibilities
⌐ ■ ■ For homework, the learners can go through their own collections and find ten or so examples of song titles with brackets. They make a list with the brackets removed. In a second lesson, group the learners by their musical taste: they test each other, dictating the titles or showing them with the brackets removed and checking each other's answers. It can be worth telling them to avoid things like *(Live Version)* or *(Remix)*!

**Connects to**
*Mischunking* (49)

# Film titles

This activity uses the learners' own knowledge of films and film titles, and introduces the theme of translating chunks in a cultural context. (You could also use book titles.)

Level ■ ■ ■    Duration ● ● ◡

## Preparation
Prepare a list of English film titles which were translated completely differently into the learners' L1. The learners need to be able to access the internet for this activity. You will also need blank A4 sheets per pair or group.

## Procedure
▫ With the learners, pool titles of English films which were translated into their L1 in an unpredictable or literal fashion, using a completely unrelated chunk. Our Polish learners came up with:

> *Dirty Dancing* = Swirling Sex / *Wirujący seks* /
> *Die Hard* = Glass Trap / *Szklana pułapka* /
> *Dirty Dozen* = Nasty Twelve / *Parszywa dwunastka* /
> *As Good As It Gets* = It Cannot Be Better / *Lepiej być nie może* /

▫ If they have problems, ask the learners to think of titles of English films in their L1 and then research the original titles in English on the Web.

▫ Divide the learners into groups to think of six more titles and research on the Web the way they were translated.

▫ Give out the A4 sheets on which the learners draw two columns – headed 'English' and 'Translation':
  ▪ In the left column, they write the English titles.
  ▪ In the right column, they write the L1 translation.

▫ They fold the sheet vertically and pass it to the next group. They can either choose to work English → L1, or L1 → English.

▫ Discuss the biggest problems they had and what chunks they have learned.

## Possibilities
❑ ■ ■ The learners might like to express their opinions about the translations – Were they *better* than the original? If they were *terrible*, can they come up with something better? You can set up an ongoing project for film translations on a notice board or designated area.

The activity can be also run as a competition, where the learners get a point for each correct translation.

**Connects to**
*L1–L2 translation* (48) ▪ *Translate that!* (40)

# Chunk in cheek

This entertaining activity raises awareness that chunks have no direct word-for-word translation. It also makes the learners aware that chunking is most probably just as prevalent in their L1 as it is in English. And it utilises their knowledge of film.

Level ■ ■ ■    Duration ● ● ◡

## Preparation
Collect a set of English chunks from a film that were 'mis-translated' into the learners' L1. Prepare a handout which shows both the original chunk and the mis-translation (see below for some examples).

## Procedure
▫ Ask the learners if they can recall bad translations when they have been watching English language films subtitled in their L1.

▫ Give out the list you have prepared. This is the beginning of a list we prepared for Polish learners:

> public school boy / *chłopak ze szkoły państwowej* / state school boy
>
> Night cap / *szlafmyca* /
> literal translation: a hat you wear in bed
>
> She will be barking / *będzie szczekać* /
> literally: barking like a dog
>
> I must go / *muszę wyjść* /
> I must go outside
>
> Duck now! / *teraz kaczka* /
> literal translation: now there is a duck
>
> Drinks on the house / *drinki na dachu* /
> drinks on the roof

▫ In pairs, the learners spot the mis-translations and suggest a better alternative.

▫ Discuss their answers with the whole class.

## Possibilities
On a notice board or designated area, you can set up an ongoing project collecting bad translations of chunks.

❑ ■ ■ You can collect and use twisted chunks which are hard to translate, and discuss the best translations, eg:
*I will have my cake and eat it.*
*What she can do with a piece of meat is rare and well done.*

**Connects to**
*Mischunking* (49) ▪ *Dictionary versus dictionary* (93)

## From English to L1

This activity raises awareness of the fact that chunks have no direct word-for-word translation. It also makes the learners aware that chunking is most probably just as prevalent in their first language as it is in English.

Level ■ ■ ■    Duration ● ● ●

### Preparation
Find an English language film with subtitles in your learners' L1. Select a suitable fragment or scene which has lexis relevant to the learners.

### Procedure
- Show the extract a first time – in English with the 'subtitles' function switched *off* – and ask the learners to remember as much as they can.
- Show the extract a second time – and ask them to write down chunks they can hear.
- Discuss the chunks they have selected – add any *you* have noticed and think are useful, writing them all on the board.
- Play the extract with the subtitles *on* – the learners notice how the selected chunks have been translated.
- Write the translations on the board – Are they correct?
- The learners memorise the L2 chunks on the board, and then you wipe the board clean.
- Play the extract once again – with the sound *off*, but the subtitles *on*. When one of the chunks you have discussed comes up, the learners have to say the English equivalent.

### Possibilities
As a follow-up, print out the transcript of the extract. Google the name of the film title followed by the word 'transcript' or go direct to a website, eg: http://www.awesomefilm.com/script/asitgets.txt. The learners can take their time and compare the transcript with the subtitles as you pause the film. Finally, they can discuss which translations they liked – and ones for which they can think of something better.

⌐ ⌐ ■ The learners can provide a running soundtrack (a simultaneous translation) rather than individual phrases. However, this makes it much more difficult as they not only have to think about the *chunks* but also the *grammar*. Also, as they say their translations, the dialogue moves on so they will miss the next bits. To avoid a neck-breaking pace, you can pause the film after an item of language you believe the learners will be able to remember – and then they translate.

**Connects to**
*Bilingual dictionaries online (41)* ▪ *Dictionary versus dictionary (93)*

## From L1 to English

As in the previous activity, here we are encouraging the learners to get away from word-for-word translation of a chunk when comparing their L1 to English.

Level ⌐ ■ ■    Duration ● ● ○

### Preparation
Find a film in your learners' language with subtitles in English. These may be harder to find than English films with L1 subtitles, but they are becoming more easily available. Select two suitable fragments with the language you want to work on, and select some chunks from the first extract.

### Procedure
- Show the first extract in the learners' L1 (*without* subtitles).
- Show the extract a second time, stopping the film when the chunks you have chosen come up.
- Ask the learners how they would translate the chunks into English.
- Show the extract a third time, *with* the English subtitles:
    - They look at how the chunks have been translated.
    - They compare with their own translations.
- Now show the *second* extract, with the English subtitles.
- Ask the learners to take some notes of the chunks they can hear – and the translations.
- Discuss if the chunks have been translated well.

### Possibilities
As an ongoing project, you can ask the learners to find their own examples of good or bad translations of chunks. The outcomes of the project can become part of a portfolio.

As a follow-up, you can ask them to identify key chunks in the translations. They can then use them to write a summary of the scene or the film.

■ ■ ■ In both of these 'translation' activities, instead of using films, you can also use *written* texts for comparing chunks in L1 and L2 – a fragment of a novel, an article or a poem and their translations. Translations may be found on the internet.

**Connects to**
*Film titles (80)*

# Chapter Five
## In data

The activities we have presented in the previous chapters of *The Company Words Keep* are based on the insights into lexical chunking gained from the study of data using programs and tools available on the Web. Here, we suggest introducing our learners to easily accessible Web resources *directly*. This can be done both in class and for their use independently outside class.

Computational linguistics utilises the two things that computers are good at: counting and sorting. The tools show the *frequency* of a word or chunk, and the *environment* in which the word or chunk is used. This data on its own is not enough – it still needs to be interpreted and discussed, and this suggests a more cooperative approach between the teacher and learners.

### Very high frequency
The first activities reintroduce the idea of corpus and concordancing to the learners. This time, however, they are encouraged to use the Web resources available directly. The aim is to find what is *frequent* – and therefore worth working with and retaining.

### Very good company
The final activities guide the learners in using Web resources to check and consolidate their knowledge of words in their *environment* – what is usefully put before and after a word to form a chunk.

The learners are encouraged to use Web resources in and out of class, including a variety of online dictionaries, the 'search' facility on the British National Corpus and also Google, which can be used as a kind of giant international corpus.

The activities in this chapter can be used:
- with the whole class – using a data projector linked to the Web;
- in small groups – if you have enough hardware and Web access;
- for homework – assuming the learners have access at home or in a library.

A fuller list of websites can be found in the 'Research' section at the end of *The Company Words Keep*.

## Chunk champion

The learners are introduced to Google as a kind of giant corpus which they can access easily, getting a picture of English as a language used by native speakers from various countries as well as non-natives. They work with Google frequency in a fun, competitive way – activating the chunks they already know.

Level ■ ■ ■      Duration ● ◡ ◡

### Preparation
You need a class with internet access for each pair of learners.

### Procedure
- Write the chunk 'my best friend' on the board and ask the learners to predict how many times it appears in Google.
- Google the chunk.
- Show the learners where the information comes up – in the upper-right-hand corner. For example:

  Results 1–10 of about 140,000,000 results (0.23 seconds)

- Divide the class into pairs and tell the learners they are going to play a game:
  - The first pair come to front.
  - Each learner writes their contribution on the board.
  - The other pairs google the chunks.
  
  The winner of the pair is the learner whose chunk appears more often.

- Continue with the second pair – and so on.
  - The winners go on to the next round, forming new pairs and coming up with new chunks.
  - The losers become observers – or become a support team.
  
  The competition carries on – to the final round.

- You announce the winner:

  *Chunk champion of the month.*

### Possibilities
Instead of coming up with chunks of their own, the learners can look through their coursebooks or other texts they have used in class.

If the class is big, the activity can be done in subgroups.

If the learners like the activity, you can repeat the contest on a regular basis – every month a new champion!

**Connects to**
*A class concordance* (42)

# Chunk quest

The learners use Google as a way to learn new, high-frequency chunks related to chunks they already know – all in a fun and visual way.

Level ■■■   Duration ●●◡

## Preparation
You need a class with internet access for each pair of learners, possibly also data projection.

## Procedure
- Ask the learners to google the phrase 'business partner'.
- They scroll down to the bottom of the page to the 'searches related to …' feature:

| Searches related to **business partner** | |
|---|---|
| business partner **wanted** | business partner **agreement** |
| **find a** business partner | business partner **synonym** |
| business partner **definition** | **ibm** business partner |
| business **partnership** | **esri** business partner **conference** |

- The learners check which of the chunks they know. They find one which is worth learning, eg 'business partner wanted', they click on the chunk, and see what comes up:

| Searches related to **business partner wanted** |
|---|
| business partner wanted **forum** |
| **get** business partner wanted |
| business partner wanted **for marketing** |
| business partner wanted **insurance** |

- Repeat the procedure a few times.
- Ask the learners to do the Google quest and keep a record of their search in the form of a chunk map. For example:

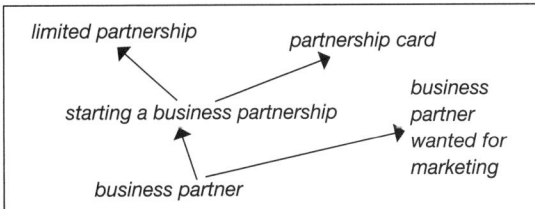

## Possibilities
You can divide the class into pairs and tell them to create similar chunk maps, starting with a chunk of their choice. Display or circulate the results.

**Connects to**
*International words* (31) ▪ *Be a sport* (38)

# Fight it out!

This activity makes the learners aware of the relationships and the differences between 'similar' words and chunks, as well as their frequency, and gets them using the internet at home for their own research.

Level ■■■   Duration ●●◡

## Preparation
Call up Googlefight on your computer and familiarise yourself with the program: *http://www.googlefight.com/*. You need a classroom with an internet connection and a data projector (or you can adapt the activity as homework).

## Procedure
- Ask the learners to decide which chunk is more common in English: *nice day* or *lovely day*?
- Have a vote, and then 'googlefight' the two chunks – see below for what the result might look like:

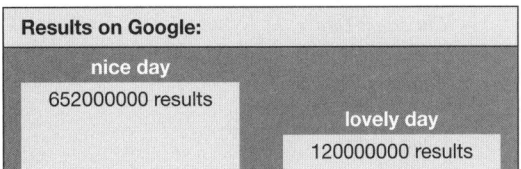

- Invite the learners to think of more related pairs of chunks.
- Give them a couple of minutes, take bets, and then googlefight the pairs of chunks they have suggested.

## Possibilities
■■■ You can prepare the chunks beforehand, setting them out on a grid so that the learners can make their predictions by putting a tick in the box. These worked well with our classes:

| Chunk 1 | Chunk 2 | |
|---|---|---|
| make money | do business | |
| the cat's whiskers | important | |
| pouring with rain | raining cats and dogs | |
| pint of lager | pint of bitter | |
| climb the career ladder | go up the rungs | |
| quarrel | fall out | |
| once upon a time | lived happily ever after | |

**Connects to**
*'Brain sludge'* (29) ▪ *Get this!* (37)

# Fight for culture

This activity aims to improve (cross-)cultural awareness in a fun way through Googlefight. It focuses on the relationships between fixed chunks related to culture.

Level ■ ■ ■   Duration ● ● ◡

## Preparation
Set up an internet connection for the lesson and a data projector, and perhaps prepare a list of the items you want to work on.

## Procedure
- Brainstorm the most common holidays around the globe (or have a list already prepared). For example:
    *Mother's Day*
    *Boxing Day*
    *Father's Day*
    *Christmas Eve*
    *Easter*
    *Christmas Day*
    *Halloween*
    *Thanksgiving*
    *Birthday*
    *Good Friday*
    *Name day*
    *Independence Day*

- Ask the learners to put some of them into pairs which, in their opinion, go together:
    *Christmas Eve / Christmas Day*
    *Easter / Good Friday*
    *Thanksgiving / Independence Day*

- Discuss their reasons, then ask the learners to decide which of the two words or chunks in the pair are more frequent. Point out that Google reflects a *global* image of culture.

- Googlefight the chunks on *http://www.googlefight.com/* and discuss the results.

- Here are some the results for the pairs above (figures change from day to day, but not the overall order):

| Christmas Eve | Christmas Day |
|---|---|
| 573000000 | 1310000000 |
| Easter | Good Friday |
| 19600000 | 740000000 |
| Thanksgiving | Independence Day |
| 22700000 | 111000000 |

## Possibilities
■ ■ ■ You can make the learners aware that film or book titles and names of authors are chunks, too – this is a good introduction to discussion of many topics. Ask them to suggest titles and give reasons why they put the two into pairs. For example:
*Winnie the Pooh / Alice in Wonderland*
*William Shakespeare / Charles Dickens*
*Hamlet / Macbeth*
*Little Red Riding Hood / Jack and the Beanstalk*
*Romeo and Juliet / Bonnie and Clyde*
*Wallace and Grommit / Tom and Jerry*

Make sure the pairs are correctly expressed, google the answers – and discuss them.

**Connects to**
*Urban dictionary online* (39)

# Chunk Bingo

This activity focuses on retrieving and practising chunks already known by learners, as well as speculating about the likelihood of certain chunks using high-frequency words. As it is a competition, the learners are very motivated and more prone to experimenting and taking risks.

Level ■■■    Duration ●●○

## Preparation
Prepare copies for yourself of a frequency list of your choice. We have used, for example:
http://www.duboislc.org/EducationWatch/First100Words.html
http://en.wikipedia.org/wiki/Most_common_words_in_English
http://wiki.answers.com/Q/Which_are_the_most_common_adverbs_in_English

## Procedure
- Tell the learners you are going to play Bingo, and ask them to draw a grid with 4 x 3 squares and write single words of their choice in the grid.
  - They should choose a variety of words, such as nouns, verbs and adjectives.
  - They should use simple words, as in the first sample card opposite.
- Tell them you are going to read a word from your frequency list.
  - They have to create a chunk including one of *their* words and the word *you* have read.
  - They can add extra words – length is not important.
  - They don't have to make a full sentence.
- Select and read aloud a word from the list, pausing after each word to give the learners a chance to come up with a likely combination, as in the second card sample.
- Play the game until one learner has completed their grid and shouts *Bingo*.
- Discuss this learner's answers, to see if there are any incorrect ones (marked * in the sample). If the learner who called *Bingo* has an incorrect answer, continue playing until the next person shouts *Bingo*.
- Repeat the discussion stage.
- Finally, the learners compare their grids in groups. Alternatively, you collect all the Bingo cards, check them and discuss the various chunks during the next lesson.

| red | shoot | work | table |
|---|---|---|---|
| from | home | I | bird |
| take | two | put | school |

| red | shoot | work | table |
|---|---|---|---|
| | *shoot time | I work all day | at the table |
| from | home | I | bird |
| take | two | put | school |

## Possibilities
You ask the learners to write only *nouns* in their grid and you dictate only *adjectives*. This will generate 'adjective–noun' combinations. This could be repeated with verbs and prepositions, nouns and nouns, nouns and adverbs, verbs and nouns: the most common combinations.

If you want to revise certain chunks such as idioms, prepare the Bingo grid yourself, and dictate words that you know go with some of the expressions – but which may not be high-frequency words.

For example, you write *frying pan*, *alarm*, and dictate the word *fire*. The learners could come up with *out of the frying pan into the fire* or *fire alarm* or *set off the fire alarm*.

---

**Connects to**
*International words* (31) ▪ *A chunky board game* (44)

## Top 20 words

This activity introduces frequency lists as a learning tool and helps the learners to be active listeners and considerate speakers – when holding a conversation, negotiating and responding to each other.

Level ■ ■ ■   Duration ● ● ◡

### Preparation
You will need copies of a frequency list (see the example below).

### Procedure
- Tell the learners that, just as there is a 'Top 20 downloads' chart, there is one for the English language.
- Put them into small groups to try to predict the 20 most common words in spoken English.
- Give them a few minutes, while you write the numbers 1–20 on the board as a list, and then proceed:
    - They give you their suggestions.
    - You consult your own list.
    - You write their suggestions in the right places when they guess correctly.
- When they have exhausted their guesses (they usually get more than half), give out the copies of the actual Top 20.

| 1 *the* | 6 *to* | 11 *er* | 16 *we* |
| 2 *I* | 7 *that* | 12 *yeah* | 17 *mm* |
| 3 *and* | 8 *a* | 13 *they* | 18 *is* |
| 4 *you* | 9 *of* | 14 *was* | 19 *know* |
| 5 *it* | 10 *in* | 15 *erm* | 20 *but* |

- Now point to these numbers:
    12 – *yeah*
    17 – *mm*
    19 – *know*
- Give the learners a chance to speculate as to why these are so frequent. Point out that:
    - *Yeah, mm* and *I know* are part of active listening ('back-channelling').
    - *Yeah, mm* and *(you) know* are part of looking after your listener ('response tokens').
- Now take a typical coursebook dialogue that the learners have recently done. Get them to add a few examples of *mm* and *yeah* and *I/you know*.
- The learners read out the dialogue, with their additions.

### Possibilities
◡ ■ ■ You can use this activity specifically to prepare examination candidates – Cambridge ESOL and others now reward 'successful' rather than 'well-formed' language in the oral part of their exams. Checking on your listener and showing you are listening, using the chunks highlighted here, should pay dividends.

■ ■ ■ There is a game which does something similar and which is easy to find on the Web:
*http://www.sporcle.com/games/common_english_words.php*
It has the Top 100 words, but our learners have enjoyed using it. It can be done by the whole class using a data projector, or in groups using the learners' own hardware. (A good homework task, too!)

We can use frequency lists to get our learners to notice features of spoken language (an idea introduced to us by Mike McCarthy).

**Connects to**
*Gossip, not communication* (65) • *Recycling a dialogue* (45)

## Top 100 collocations

Raising awareness of which chunks are the most common and useful to learn and use will help to review key concepts from previous activities from this book – looking after your listener, active listening, hedging, softeners, politeness, etc.

Level ▫▪■    Duration ●●●

### Preparation
Prepare copies of the Top 100 Collocations in spoken English. You can find it on the Web in an ELTJ article: *http://eltj.oxfordjournals.org/content/62/4/339.full?ijkey=ShSF KiZcqeidYtm&keytype=ref*. (The full article is 'Beyond single words: the most frequent collocations in spoken English' by Dongkwang Shin and Paul Nation.)

### Procedure
- Ask the learners to turn an A4 piece of paper lengthways and divide it into eight columns.
- Dictate the eight items below, asking the learners to put one at the head of each column. (The eighth column is for those collocations that they will be unsure of.)
- They should have this list – spread over the columns:
  1. Looking after your listener/ active listening
  2. Hedging
  3. Softener/vagueness
  4. Quantity
  5. Time
  6. Place/direction
  7. Negative/positive politeness
  8. Not sure
- Check that the learners are familiar with the concepts, and give out copies of the Top 100 Collocations.
- In threes, the learners work through the list, discuss the pragmatic use of the collocation and place it in the appropriate column. (Make it clear that some will have more than one possible answer and that the eighth column is for those that they are not sure of.)
- Stop after they have had a reasonable amount of time and discuss their conclusions so far.
- Finally, let them do the rest for homework, or in class if you have enough time.

### Possibilities
Alternatively, you can divide the class into five groups and give each group 20 of the Top 100. They exchange their results, or research on the BNC to check their answers

You can also simply give out the list of the 100 and ask the learners to come up with their own categories.

**Connects to**
*From culture to culture* (68) ▪ *Gossip, not communication* (65)

## Opinion versus data

When learners have mis-learnt something from a book, it is difficult to convince them you are right and they are wrong. Cooperating in research is an excellent way to introduce the benefits of corpus linguistics and Web resources – and to show that *data* is more important than *opinion*.

Level ▪■■    Duration ●◐◐

### Preparation
This is 'point of need' grammar teaching, and works well as a response to a concern that learners express in class. The problem highlighted below was a direct response to learner uncertainties – no preparation is possible, therefore.

### Procedure
- Be on the lookout for problem areas that the learners are unconvinced or uncertain about. For example:

  Paul: *'My class had got it into their heads that you had to say 'have a bath/shower'; 'take a bath/shower' was wrong. This was due to their previous encounter with a syllabus. I was pretty sure that both were OK and said so – but they seemed to remain a bit unconvinced.'*

- If you have data projection, call up the British National Corpus or Googlefight and type in the query (if not, you set it for homework and the learners can research it at home). Here are the results of the occurrences for our delexified verb example above:

| BNC | | Googlefight | |
|---|---|---|---|
| have a shower | 48 | have a shower | 45,200,000 |
| take a shower | 22 | take a shower | 13,400,000 |
| have a bath | 145 | have a bath | 70,000,000 |
| take a bath | 26 | take a bath | 29,500,000 |

- Discuss the results. It seems here from the data that *both* are possible, but the learners were right – in the sense that 'have' is much more common. (Note, too, that further corpus research will show that 'have' is more commonly *spoken* English, 'take' more formal or literary.)

### Possibilities
■ ■ ■ This is a good technique for dealing with quibbles from individual learners. It is often the more disaffected learners who are technophiles, and it is a good way of 'including' those who are not normally very motivated or have different learning styles. It is also a way for the *teacher* to learn!

**Connects to**
*Old words, new partnerships* (73)

# Complete the collocation

The learners discover how to research chunks using Google when they feel that there must be a chunk but they cannot think of it or are not sure if they remember it correctly. This activity is particularly suitable for writing activities, as learners need time to do their online research.

Level ⬜ ◼ ◼    Duration ● ● ◡

## Preparation
You will need data projection and a computer with internet access per pair or group of three learners.

## Procedure
- Write the following on the board:

    *I would like to welcome you*

- Ask the learners to suggest how to finish the sentence and write up their suggestions.

- Call up Google, and type in:

    *I would like to welcome you**

- Scroll down the first few pages. Ask the learners to note down the different ways in which the sentences can be *completed* – by focusing on the various chunks. They will come up with something like the examples in the first box opposite.

- Scroll down the same pages a second time. This time, ask the learners to notice any useful chunks which go *before* the sentence stem. See the second box opposite.

- Finally, ask the class in what ways they could use this facility to help them with their writing, for example when preparing a speech.

## Possibilities
The next time the learners have a written task or have to prepare a talk for class, ask them to use the facility and then comment on how effective it was.

⬜ ◼ ◼ You can come up with your own expressions, work with learners' suggestions or work with sentences from the coursebook. The activity above suggests using a *chunk* as a starting point – but a *key word* can also throw up interesting search results.

---

*I would like to welcome you* sincerely to the Saint Petersburg Economic Conference

*I would like to welcome you* to something new in UC faculty communications

*I would like to welcome you* guys to come to my blog

*I would like to welcome you* all

*I would like to welcome you* to another exciting season of McMaster football

*I would like to welcome you* back

---

Ladies and gentlemen, *I would like to welcome you*

On behalf of … *I would like to welcome you*

Dear colleagues, *I would like to welcome you*

My staff and *I would like to welcome you*

First, *I would like to welcome you*

---

**Connects to**
*Expansion* (46) ▪ *Chunks first, then grammar* (50)

# Friendly facilities

The learners become familiar with available online concordancers as a more sophisticated tool than the BNC simple search. They learn what kind of information they can get, how to choose different options and how to interpret the results – making friends with concordances.

Level ■ ■ ■   Duration ● ● ○

## Preparation
Prepare an example of a concordance, and print it out or use data projection (see the example opposite). A good site is: *http://www.lextutor.ca/concordancers/concord_e.html*. Also, find three different concordances of an easy word of your choice using the facility: 'equals', 'starts' and 'contains'. Prepare copies of each. Make sure you have done the activities *A class concordance* and *Learner concordances* (page 42) first.

## Procedure
- Remind the learners of *A class concordance* and *Learner concordances*, checking they remember that, in a concordance, the key word is in a central position.
- As a warm-up and to review the idea of corpus, give out an example of a concordance like the one opposite for 'walk' – and ask the learners to study it.
- Discuss what they notice, confirming or clarifying.
- Divide the class into three groups and give out the three concordances you have prepared, a different one to each group. See opposite.
- Ask the groups to decide what information they get from their concordance – they might comment on word partnerships or word order, for example.
- Regroup the learners in different threes, so that each previous group is represented, and ask them to compare their observations on a *different* concordance of the *same* word. They should find *similarities* as well as *differences*.
- Discuss their observations with the whole class.

## Possibilities
▯ ■ ■ The learners can compare the results of their findings with dictionary entries of the word. This should lead them into a discussion of how good their dictionary is – and whether they need a new, corpus-based one!

The learners find their own concordances for homework – this research could be themed around a coursebook topic.

**walk**

, let's you and me go for **a WALK** down by the Snake- all by
Marv Throneberry drew **a WALK** and stole second as Hyde
like this: Lumpe worked **a WALK** as the first batter to face H
to take her home. It was **a WALK** up on Hudson Street. She j
irs, a concrete floor, and **a WALK**-way along the upper side i
air; and, when you took **a WALK** you never knew what adve
Lighting my pipe, I took **a WALK**. The Harbor is a big yachti
reath; then he slowed to **a WALK**. The vision became even s

**'equals'**

ies sighed and remarked, "**WISH** I was 40, and a top-grade b
-director, had expressed **a WISH** that Anthony Payne drop de
ost fleeting fragment of **a WISH** to know, for the fact that on
on and the possibility of **a WISH** to identify his own life with t
tresses on emeralds **and WISH**; note pitch 3 (pretty high) or
mbolized **Mrs. Coolidge's WISH** for a little girl. Among the d
sely vibrant as one **could WISH**, almost an icy shriek threate
d wish that. Or you **could WISH** your daddy would really do

**'starts'**

n closing, Mr. Barcus **also WISH**ed all the Juniors luck in thei
assented. Had he **always WISH**ed to be a conductor? No, o
d Australia (Clements **and WISH**art, 1956). There it seems th
rry for independence **and WISH**ed to wait until the Congo gr
smissed these feelings **as WISH**ful thinking but I could not g
whenever the younger **boy WISH**ed. The two of them had de
nder a big canvas **cover.) WISH**ing to show that aviation wa
be required. If a **customer WISH**es a special cut, it will not b

**'contains'**

-director, had expressed **a WISH** that Anthony Payne drop de
ost fleeting fragment of **a WISH** to know, for the fact that on
ion and the possibility of **a WISH** to identify his own life with t
ul suspend itself above **all WISH**ing and desire. She did this
n closing, Mr. Barcus **also WISH**ed all the Juniors luck in thei
assented. Had he **always WISH**ed to be a conductor? No, o
lopments in **American-Je WISH** life is that the cultural consu
d you could sit all day **and WISH** it would spring a leak or blo

---

**Connects to**
*Going for a song* (91) ▪ *A class concordance* (42)

## Google the chunk

The learners expand the chunks they know containing a given word. The activity also gets them to focus on looking at the environment of a word: what comes *before* and *after*. It is a good preparation for using concordancers.

Level ☐ ■ ■    Duration ● ● ◡

### Preparation
You will need an internet connection and data projection.

### Procedure
- Write the word 'master' on the board, and ask the learners what chunks they can come up with.
- Call up Google, and type in: *master. You will get something like the following:

  ```
  *master
  master cleanse
  master cook
  masterlease
  mastercard
  ```

- In pairs, the learners say what lexical area they think the phrases come from: *university*, *business*, etc.
- If they are uncertain about any of the chunks, scroll down and click on it. You will get some examples of the word in context. For example, with *master cleanse*:

  > The *Master Cleanse* is such a simple program …
  > A modified juice fast that permits no food …

- Repeat the procedure with: *master* (no asterisk) and *master** (followed by an asterisk). You will get slightly different results.

  ```
  master              master*
  mastercook          master of puppets
  masterlease         mastercard
  masters             master of science
  mastercard          master sport
  ```

- Get the learners to notice what new chunks have appeared, then discuss which of the chunks are useful to them – and therefore worth learning.

### Possibilities
☐ ■ ■ The learners can work in groups and work on words that they choose themselves. They research the chunks on Google, then share their discoveries with other groups.

**Connects to**
*Pass the chunk* (34) • *Be a sport* (38)

---

## From chunks to sentences

Putting chunks into sentences is a crucial writing skill – here, the learners construct sentences from fragments listed in concordances, contextualising the lexical items.

Level ☐ ■ ■    Duration ● ● ◡

### Preparation
Prepare a concordance of a word suitable for your class and make copies for all the learners. You may trim it by removing words to the right or left – see the example below.

### Procedure
- Remind the learners of the way concordances are written.
- Give out the concordance you have selected, or use the sample text below.
- Ask the learners to (re)construct a whole sentence (or clause) which is included in the concordance but, due to the nature of concordances, is presented incompletely:

  > promised to pay her a **LUMP** sum in lieu of
  > found a **LUMP** rising in his throat

- Our learners produced the following:

  > *When she was let go, they promised to pay her a lump sum in lieu her pension but they never did.*
  > *As Tom read his test results he found a lump rising in his throat.*

- The learners compare their sentences. They can also decide what *kind* of text the sentences come from.
- If you have data projection, you can access the original sentence and compare it with the learners' sentences by clicking on the key word:

  > At the time of her divorce Forbes had promised to pay her a lump sum in lieu of further alimony if she remarried.
  > He found a lump rising in his throat because of that one simple act of tidiness.

### Possibilities
☐ ■ ■ The learners can work in groups, each group getting a different set of concordances. After they have written their own sentences, the sets circulate from group to group. The learners read the sentences and identify the key word or chunk the other group was working with. They also check if the new sentences are grammatically correct.

**Connects to**
*Chunks first, then grammar* (50)

# Going for a song

Lines from songs are an excellent source of memorable chunks, reflecting the learners' interests and often known 'unconsciously' to them, anyway. This activity reinforces the idea of pooling examples of chunks in the layout of a concordance created by the learners themselves.

Level    Duration

## Preparation

Get references to one or two websites which give song lyrics. For example:

*http://www.elyrics.net*
*http://search.azlyrics.com*
*http://www.lyricsmode.com*

You will need a computer for each pair of learners or group of three. (Alternatively, this can be done as homework on their home computers.)

## Procedure

- Remind the learners of the idea of concordances – about alignment and layout – and tell them that they are going to research a word (our example below is 'money') and make their own concordance, using song lyrics:
    - They have to find a variety of examples of the uses of the word.
    - They will cut and paste them to make a concordance.
    - They need to aim for 15 *different* examples to get enough variety.

- Finally, discuss with the learners what they have found out about the word *money*.
  There are three distinct different patterns:
  1 verb + *money*
  2 adjective + *money*
  3 other

## Possibilities

■ ■ ■ You may want the learners to research a *grammar structure* which you are about to teach. This will make learning the grammar structure much easier.

You can show your learners that researching language does not have to be limited to academics and lexicographers (this fun activity was inspired by Vaughn Jones and Sue Kay in their course *Inside Out – Intermediate*).

They can use the websites that will search for chunks, like *http://www.lyricsmode.com*, and investigate, for example, binomials for themselves. They type in the full binomial or an incomplete binomial (for example, dropping what follows the word 'and') to see what the various possibilities are.

---

If I had more money honey, Would you love me, love me, love me
It ain't easy to make money
So now everybody wanna take money (Uh huh, uh huh)
You ain't a thug, matter fact you a fake money
Money, money, money must be funny in the rich man's world
Honey, whaddya do for money?
Dirty money, Dirty tricks
Blood money, you got blood on your hands
If money talks, it's not talkin' to me, if money talks, I said
And man it hurts to give the money away
I need money, that's what I want

---

**Connects to**
*A class concordance* (42)  ▪  *Be a sport* (38)

# The tip of the iceberg

The learners become aware of how much information they can find in dictionaries, and they also get to use metalanguage.

Level    Duration ● ● ○

## Preparation
You will need a set of monolingual corpus-based dictionaries or you can use the learners' own.

## Procedure
- Brainstorm what the learners know about icebergs:
    - If a learner gives the fact that only one ninth of the iceberg is above water, reinforce it.
    - If not, tell them.
- Draw a quick sketch of an iceberg on the board, making sure that the design is the right proportion – one part above water, eight parts underneath.
- Write *word* at the tip of the iceberg.
- Brainstorm what information the learners can find in a dictionary about a word. Encourage them to use the metalanguage they know – *part of speech*, *pronunciation*, *countable/uncountable*, *collocation*, etc.
- Write their suggestions on the iceberg, in the 'above the water level' section.
- Ask them to look through the dictionaries for more to add.
- Discuss with the whole class, and write the results of their findings *below* the water level. The final product may look like Box 1.
- Divide the learners into pairs and ask them to draw an iceberg. Make sure the proportions are right.
    - They choose an English word and write it at the tip.
    - You collect and redistribute the drawings.
- Each pair writes the chunks they know containing the key word above the water level. Further use of resources is *not allowed* at this stage.
- You collect and redistribute the drawings a second time.
- Now give out the dictionaries and *allow* access to resources. The learners research and write the new information they find below the water level. For a possible final outcome for the word *party*, see Box 2.
- Display the drawings and discuss the results. Point out how many chunks are 'below the water level'.

## Possibilities
The learners can now use this technique to do ongoing research on their own.

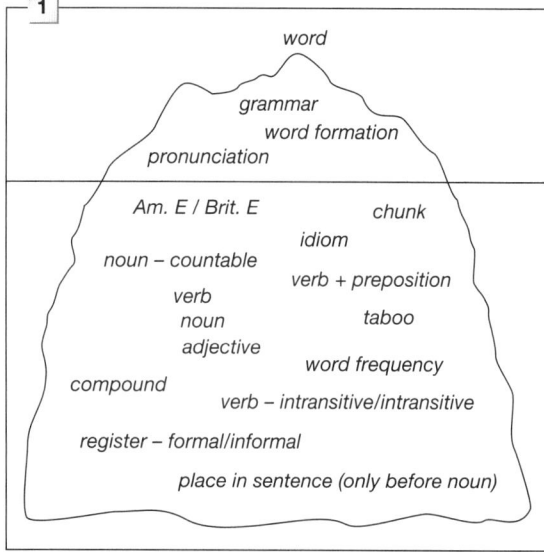

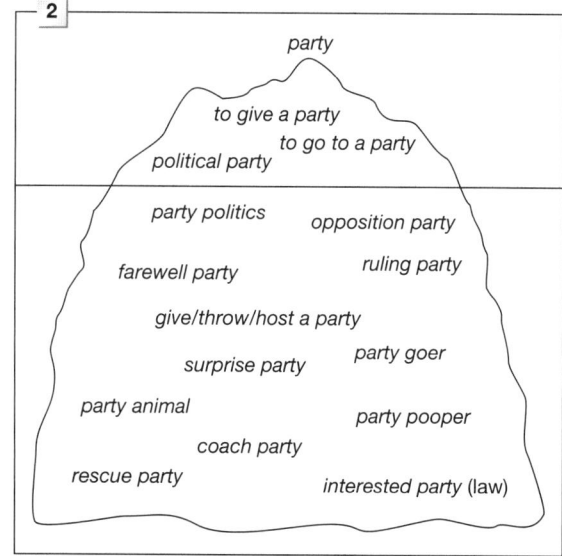

**Connects to**
*Bilingual dictionaries online* (41) ▪ *Be a sport* (38)

## Dictionary versus dictionary

This activity helps the learners to use various online dictionaries and to form opinions about which dictionaries are better for looking up chunks in translation.

Level ⊔ ■ ■     Duration ● ● ○

### Preparation
Research which suitable bilingual dictionaries (English–L1 and L1–English) are available online. Copy a full list and prepare a handout for each learner. Also prepare a card for each group with one of the website addresses. Each group will need internet access. (Alternatively, you can adapt the activity as homework.)

### Procedure
- Put the learners into groups of three around a computer, and give each group a card with one of the different websites you have chosen, and a blank sheet of paper to write their research on.
- The learners visit the website and find three English chunks for which they are not sure of the exact meaning and would find difficult to translate – even though they might know the individual words in the chunks.
- They copy the three chunks they have selected on the sheet under the website address. For example:
    http://www.bioling.com/
    *abdominal and pelvic pain*
    *anorexia nervosa*
    *malformation of coronary vessels*
    http://www.narzedziownie.pl/?t=1
    *storage battery*
    *surface finish*
    *master switch*
- The learners pass their sheet to another group, who have to try to come up with their own translation in their L1. They then look it up in the website dictionary to check.
- Shuffle and repeat the procedure.
- For homework, give out the full list of websites and ask the learners to research them. In a subsequent class, ask for their opinions about the best website dictionary.

### Possibilities
⊔ ■ ■ The learners find three chunks around a word in the dictionary but, this time, *in their L1*. They copy the chunks and pass the sheets to the next group, who have to offer a translation and then find the chunks *in English* on the website.

**Connects to**
*Chunk for chunk* (48) ▪ *Bilingual dictionaries online* (41)

## Picture this!

This activity uses Google Images as a way of researching chunks around a key word. The 'search images' feature combines the lexical with the visual and helps the learners, especially at lower levels, to research and remember chunks through images by doing a mini-project.

Level ■ ■ ■     Duration ● ○ ○

### Preparation
Prepare a list of words you would like to work on. You will need internet access with data projection or internet access for each pair of learners and a printer (or the activity could be adapted for homework).

### Procedure
- Select a word the learners have come across recently. For example: *gown*.
- Google the word – and choose the 'Images' function.
- Go through the pictures with the learners, and count how many different types of gowns they can see.
- Discuss the various chunks in which the word appears in the captions.
- Create a file with different images and captions. These are some of the examples we found:

> prom dance star **gown**
> bridal **gown**
> custom JD doctoral **gown**
> pediatric **gown**
> cotton chambray dressing **gown**
> brushed cotton white **gown**
> infant **gown**
> embroidered crest christening **gown**
> large EFP ultra protection **gown**
> Arab **gown**
> labor and delivery **gowns**

- Now put the learners into pairs and allocate different words to each pair.
- The pairs carry out their image search and prepare a file with their findings (this can be done in class if you have enough computers, otherwise for homework).
- Print out the learners' work and circulate it.

### Possibilities
The sheets can be circulated, displayed on the wall or posted online as an ongoing project.

**Connects to**
*Learner concordances* (42) ▪ *Urban dictionary online* (39)

# Picture dictionaries online

This activity makes the learners aware of how many chunks they can find in picture dictionaries – they look at pictures to expand their knowledge of chunks around a particular topic. Visuals and drawing are both fun, and appeal to the visual learners in the class.

## Preparation
Find a website picture dictionary suitable for your learners, eg *http://visual.merriam-webster.com/*.

You need internet access and enough computers to put the learners in groups of three around a computer. (If not, the activity can be set for homework.)

## Procedure
- Divide the class into groups of three around a computer, and call up the dictionary menu. For example: *http://visual.merriam-webster.com/about-visual_overview.php*

  - Astronomy
  - Earth
  - Plants & gardening
  - Animal kingdom
  - Human being
  - Food & kitchen
  - House
  - Clothing & articles
  - Arts & architecture
  - Communications
  - Transport & machinery
  - Energy
  - Science
  - Society
  - Sports & games

- Ask each group to choose one topic area from the menu, give out A4 sheets of paper and ask the learners write their topic at the top.

- Each group designs a quest for the other groups – to find pictures of three chunks. For example:

  | Clothing | Astronomy |
  |---|---|
  | *drop earrings* | *outer planets* |
  | *twin set* | *inner planets* |
  | *short sleeve* | *celestial bodies* |

- Give the learners a two-minute time limit, then ask them to pass their quiz to the group on their right:
  - The group has to find a picture for each chunk.
  - The best 'artist' in each group makes a quick sketch of the visual on the paper to show they have found the right image – and to add some fun to the activity! It makes the chunks more memorable as the students make the images their own, this way.

- They then add to the list three *new* chunks from the same topic area that have to be found and write them on the same piece of paper.

- The next group finds the pictures and make drawings – and so on.

- Once the word list and drawings have filled the sheet, stop the activity and display the results.

## Possibilities
With higher levels, you can go to the main page (*http://visual.merriam-webster.com/*) where you will find icons with the topic areas.
- Ask the learners to choose one of the topics and brainstorm the chunks they think they know.
- Make sure you keep a count of the chunks and write the number on the board.
- Check against the chunks that appear as key words on the site. For example:
  *http://visual.merriam-webster.com/astronomy.php*
  And then on respective sub-sites. For example:
  *http://visual.merriam-webster.com/astronomy/celestial-bodies.php*
- Get the learners to say which chunks they *knew* but they did not *come up with*. Keep count of these chunks.
- Compare with the original figure you have written on the board. This tends to show the learners that they know more than they think they know.

**Connects to**
*Draw a chunk* (43)

# Word sketch

The learners work with information that is used to create a dictionary entry and look at which verbs frequently come *before* and *after* a particular noun, and how words collocate with the key word. 'Word sketches' are used as a tool by lexicographers and are concordances organised according to the frequency and environment of a word.

Level   Duration

## Preparation

Choose a key word linked to the topic that the learners are working on; our example is for the word 'waiter'. Go to: *www.sketchengine.co.uk* and ask for a word sketch of the word. You can print out the tables, but the grids, as they appear on the screen, are quite cluttered – so it may be preferable to prepare simplified handouts as in the example opposite. Alternatively, have data projection ready for use.

## Procedure

- Write the word you have chosen on the board. For example: 'waiter'.
- Ask the learners the following question: *What do waiters do?* Write up a few answers: *waiters bring food*; *waiters serve* …
- Now ask the learners: *What do you do with the waiter?* Get a few answers: *call the waiter*; *ask the waiter to* …
- Keep a record of their suggestions.
- Now show the word profile you have prepared (either give out copies or use a data projector) and ask the learners to find the words they have suggested.
- Discuss how the words in the grid and the key word collocate, and what other words are added.
- The word sketch shows verbs that commonly *precede* or *follow* the word 'waiter'. The learners will see that you are much more likely to *summon* (9) or *call* (10) a waiter than *beckon* (5) or *signal* (5).
- The learners should make phrases containing the word *waiter* and the other high-frequency words that collocate with it. They should go for the high numbers.

| object of | |
|---|---|
| summon | 9 |
| beckon | 5 |
| signal | 5 |
| call | 10 |
| ask | 6 |
| tell | 6 |
| say | 9 |

| subject of | |
|---|---|
| hover | 7 |
| bring | 24 |
| arrive | 12 |
| come | 27 |
| serve | 10 |
| pour | 5 |
| approach | 5 |
| stand | 7 |
| appear | 7 |
| look | 8 |
| take | 8 |
| say | 9 |
| go | 5 |
| make | 6 |

## Possibilities

The learners can note down the website for future reference and use it for speaking and writing about a topic. At the time of writing, the site *www.sketchengine.co.uk* was available free for the first month, after which a fee is charged. A free alternative is: *http://corpus.byu.edu/bnc/*.

**Connects to**
*Building around a chunk* (49) • *Chunks first, then grammar* (50)

# Your last chance

Learners need to recognise word partnerships and their
'strength' – for example, knowing the word *chance* is rather
useless without knowing the relationships it has with other
words. Some of these are more 'likely' than others,
and learners need to develop an 'inner criteria' of
what works and what does not.

Level  Duration ● ● ◡

## Preparation
Choose a suitable word and prepare copies of the definition from a good corpus-based dictionary, or have dictionaries to hand in class.

## Procedure
- Ask the learners to take a completely blank sheet of paper and turn it lengthways.
- They write *likely* on the **left** and *unlikely* on the **right**:
- Dictate half a dozen easy samples, to warm the class up. For example: *strong coffee, soft drink, heavy coffee, heavy lunch, soft drugs, light drugs*. (The examples at this stage should be easy, since the aim is simply to get the idea.)
- Ask the learners, working alone, to write your examples towards the *left* if they see them as strong, *likely* combinations of words – or towards the *right* if they see them as weak, *unlikely* combinations of words:

```
       S T R O N G                    W E A K
L        strong coffee      light drugs          U
I        soft drink                              N
K                                                L
E                           heavy coffee         I
L        heavy lunch                             K
Y        soft drugs                              E
                                                 L
                                                 Y
```

- Give the learners a few moments to discuss with their neighbours and, if necessary, check with the whole class.
- Now dictate the following, again asking the learners to place the examples on their continuum, depending on how strong they feel the partnership is:

  *light chance   slim chance   slight chance   fat chance
  strong chance   heavy chance   good chance   fair chance*

  (The quicker the dictation the better. With this kind of judgement, the learners' first thought is usually the best.)

- When you have finished dictating, ask the learners to compare their notes in pairs.
- As they are checking, distribute the copies of the dictionary definition of 'chance' (or hand out the dictionaries) so they can check their answers. Don't answer any questions at this stage – simply refer the learners to the copy.
- When they have checked their answers, end with a discussion about how useful the dictionary was.
  □ In the full Macmillan English Dictionary which we were using, the learners can successfully research this activity with *chance*. For example: *fat chance* is in but *heavy chance* isn't.
  □ Their *online* dictionary is not extensive enough and neither is the *student* edition of the Macmillan dictionary.

This activity will only work with a good unabridged corpus-based dictionary.

## Possibilities
⬜ ■ ■ *Chance* is one of the most frequent words in the corpus (among the most common 1000 words in English, according to *http://www.englishclub.com/vocabulary/common-words-5000.htm*. You can usefully repeat this activity with other frequent words which 'work hard', words like *place, stuff, thing, relationship*. (See a frequency list from a corpus for more common nouns, or check in a corpus-based dictionary – frequent nouns are starred red in the Macmillan English Dictionary, for example.)

These types of collocational questions put an awful lot of pressure on teachers to come up with the 'right' answer off the top of their head. Realistically, good cooperation between learners and teacher in researching the correct answer – plus a good dictionary – is the only answer.

**Connects to**
*Vocabulary lists* (41) ▪ *Chunks first, then grammar* (50)

# Questions, queries and quibbles

The first activities in this chapter approached Google as a kind of giant corpus. This final set of activities in Part B of *The Company Words Keep* uses a specific corpus – the British National Corpus (BNC) – to conclude our exploration of using data in language learning. The corpus enables you:
- to answer questions which you might have as a teacher;
- to respond at point of need to queries and quibbles your learners might ask;
- to encourage the learners to access the corpus directly – and investigate for themselves.

Space here only permits us to outline a few areas where you will find the BNC useful – but the possibilities are vast. Both you *and* your learners can investigate mistakes that tend to be made, words that tend to be confused, words that are wrongly associated exclusively with certain grammatical forms, small words which seem insignificant and are often overlooked but which are highly important …

A few pointers:
- The BNC is 200 million words of mainly British English.
- It is rather like having all the utterances of a native speaker over a lifetime 'on tap'.
- It is more *written* than *spoken* English, but it deals pretty well with queries about spoken English.
- The simple search facility gives a straightforward and user-friendly guide to the *frequency* of a chunk and also its *environment* (what comes before and after).
- Besides the simple search on the BNC site, there are many more options suitable for class research.
- If you are interested in American English, check the Research section at the end of *The Company Words Keep* for websites.
- If you are interested in more sophisticated programs – that compare American with British English, spoken with written, that compare genres, and so on – then check, also, the Research section for appropriate sites.

Enjoy!

## Frequency

The learners are introduced to the British National Corpus and the idea of using a simple search of a corpus to get insights into the frequency and use of specific chunks.

### Preparation

Select a small problem for the learners to solve (see below). Decide how you are going to use the media – there are three possibilities:
- Use a data projector connected to the Web with the whole class if you have one.
- Get the learners to check on their own laptops/mobiles in class time.
- Get the learners to check for homework and bring the data back to class.

Familiarise yourself with the simple search facility of the British National Corpus (BNC) at *www.natcorp.ox.ac.uk* (it's free to access and very easy to use).

### Procedure

- Write on the board: *have dinner / eat dinner*
- Pair the learners and ask them 'Which?'
- Bring the class together and get their ideas – there is usually a degree of disagreement about when one or the other is used. Using the simple search, look up how frequent the chunks are in the BNC. This is shown at the top of the screen.

  (The results we got were: *eat dinner* 7 / *have dinner* 117)

- Ask the learners to comment on the data – ie there is a strong tendency to use *have dinner* rather than *eat dinner* in British English.

### Possibilities

You can also familiarise yourself with the search facility of the American Corpus of Contemporary English (COCA) at *www.corpus.byu.edu/coca* (it's free if you register, and quite easy to use). Repeat the search procedure then ask the learners to compare the British and American results.

You can use the search facility to settle questions in class which you or a student are not sure about.

The *take/have a bath* example used earlier (page 87) is based on an argument in one of our classes. It is difficult, off the top of your head, to give a definitive answer – going directly to the data makes a useful learner training activity.

This type of activity is also useful for dealing with individual quibbles. If a learner challenges you, refer them to the search – and ask them to get data for themselves!

## Environment

By using a simple search of a corpus, the learners can get data on the environment of a word. Corpus examples provide insight into, and deal with, persistent mistakes.

### Preparation

Identify a lexical area that is a problem for your learners. Visit the BNC website (*www.natcorp.ox.ac.uk*) and copy and print out or project examples from the simple search.

If necessary, limit the number of sentences, choosing them according to the learners' level, and prepare copies for each learner.

### Procedure

- Tell the learners of a problem area you have noticed, eg when they produce the sentence '*He/she made a career*'. (Our learners often use this to say what profession someone is in, rather than meaning 'succeeded in a chosen profession'.)

  ▶ See page 100.

- Give out the copies with your sentences from the corpus. Ask the learners to underline the phrase '*make a career*' and notice what words it is often preceded or followed by.

- Discuss the findings.

### Possibilities

Instead of a lexical item which the learners have problems with, you can choose a seemingly ordinary, straightforward word like *cat* or like *place*.

This may seem very simple, but a word like *place* has many different nuances and meanings, especially in contrast to the learners' first language; *cat* is also more complex than it first appears to be!

## Genre

Learners often lack an authentic context for lexical items. In this activity, they encounter the same item a number of times in an authentic context, becoming familiar with the corpus and the simple search tool for classroom and private use.

### Preparation

Choose a word your learners tend to have problems with (we have chosen *occasion*, which is often misused or confused with 'chance' or 'opportunity'.). Visit the simple search website (*www.natcorp.ox.ac.uk*) and copy or print out examples.

If necessary, limit the number of sentences, selecting them according to the learners' level. Make sure a variety of genres is represented, eg newspapers, literature, spoken English, academic writing, etc, and prepare copies for each learner.

### Procedure

- Discuss the idea of genre with the learners, to see what they already know.

- Explain that they will be working on authentic sentences that come from different genres. Give out the handout you have prepared.

  ▶ See page 100.

- Ask the learners to identify what source the sentences come from – newspaper, novel, etc. Can they give more details, eg serious newspaper, sport section, romantic novel, and so on? Discuss their answers.

- Ask the learners to look at the sentences again, and underline the word *occasion*.

- They work in pairs and come up with what context/environment the word *occasion* is used in and its precise meaning, eg 'one time', 'an important event', 'sometimes'.

- As homework, you can ask the learners to research the words *chance* and *opportunity* for themselves.

### Possibilities

In the activity above, the learners are speculating. If you think it is a good idea to give them the actual source, you may look it up by clicking on the blue underlined number on the left of each entry:

> AJJ **220** On the only occasion he was beaten he finished a go

When examining the sources the sentences come from, the learners can be asked to give further, more specific details:
- serious newspaper, popular newspaper, tennis section, football pages
- romantic novel, 19th century novel, historical novel
- science fiction, non-fiction
- formal letter, informal letter, diary
- journal, manual, magazine, scientific, medical

## Grammar

This inductive approach to grammar invites the learners to discover the rule before they encounter it in the coursebook. It shows the relationship between chunks and grammar, and introduces priming and colligation – how lexis moulds and influences grammar.

### Preparation

Prepare a handout for each learner of the results of a search of a target structure.

### Procedure

- Distribute the handout and ask the learners to observe in what grammar context the chunk '*If I were you ...*' appears, for example.

▶ See page 100.

- The learners compare their observations. Ask them if they can generate a rule about the use of *'If I were you …'*.
- They compare their findings with the grammar information in their coursebook or in a grammar book.

## Possibilities

Instead of a lexical item, you may want to choose a 'grammar word', eg *will*. The learners have to identify what use of *will* they come across in each sentence, eg future reference, future development which cannot be avoided, prediction, first conditional. At higher levels, this is a good review; at lower levels, it can be used to introduce a new grammar structure.

You can choose a word or phrase normally associated with an item of grammar, eg 'since' – *present perfect tense*. Ask the learners to study the sentences. In how many cases is *since* connected with the present perfect tense? In how many cases does 'since' occur in contexts *other* than the present perfect?

# Colligation

The learners look at grammar and lexis interacting. They discover that small, grammatically loaded words such as prepositions show that colligation (lexis and grammar combining to form a chunk) is as important as are lexical combinations.

## Preparation

Select a couple of 'small' words. For example: *for* and *by*, which are important grammatically but often neglected by coursebooks and grammar books. Prepare a printout of a search. Prepare copies for each learner plus copies of the information given on the words in the books that they normally use.

## Procedure

- Divide the class into two equal groups ('by' and 'for') and allocate a word to each group to research.
- Give out the lists of sentences to the appropriate groups.
- Explain that, working alone, they have to underline their word and the *whole chunk* the word is part of.
  (They don't need to understand the full sentence: just the chunks that form the environment of the key word.)
- Ask the learners to get into pairs within their group and compare the results of their work. What kind of grammar structures or grammatical tenses do the words go with?
- Regroup the class – learners from the 'by' group and the 'for' group exchange and discuss their findings.
- Give out the handouts with information on the word you have taken from their coursebooks or grammar books. They compare their findings with the information there.

▶ See page 100.

## Possibilities

You can choose to work on a pair of words that are often confused, eg *house* vs *home* or *journey* vs *travel*. Ask the learners to use the simple search examples to generate the rule for correct usage.

# Register

Here, the learners look at similar chunks with different registers – to notice that apparently similar words require a different environment: in this case, what works with 'telly' doesn't always work with 'TV'.

## Preparation

Prepare a handout with sentences from a simple search for the chunks you want to work on. See the samples on the next page for *in front of the telly / in front of the TV*.

## Procedure

- Write on the board the chunks:
  *in front of the telly / in front of the TV*
- Ask the learners to brainstorm what verbs or phrases precede or follow these chunks and write them up:

| look forward to a nice evening | sleep |
| mesmerised | sit | all day long |
| brooding on the past | couch potatoes sitting |

- Give out the sentences you have prepared. Ask the learners to research the environment in which the chunks occur and how they collocate, and underline the relevant items.
- Discuss the learners' observations – Do they notice any differences between the seemingly identical chunks?

▶ See page 100.

## Possibilities

The learners can choose their own chunks and research them as homework. In class, they report their findings.

At higher levels, you may want to research the chunks *in front of the telly* and *in front of the TV* with regard to a series of specific words: *sprawled, plonked, curled up, installed, slumped, lounge, vegetate …*

▶ Remember: the examples from the British National Corpus included on page 100 are random samples. Each time you access the BNC, you will see a different set of 50 examples (if available) – in random order.

**Frequency**

Your query was:
*make a career*

**A17** 1543 Keith Waugh has managed to make a career in the RAF a family concern – and is making a tremendous success of it.

**ADP** 447 I wanted to make a career for myself outside Salzburg.

**AT1** 591 They managed to avoid the panning reserved for contemporaries like Bogshed who were termed: 'Four twisted misanthropes trying to make a career out of sneering at people' by Dave Jennings in the NME.

**Genre**

Your query was:
*occasion*

**ABR** 596 In 1980–1, in the first Test to be played on his home ground in Antigua, there was never any doubt that he was going to mark the occasion with a century, and, as we shall see, when England returned five years later he marked that occasion in the most spectacular fashion.

**AJJ** 220 On the only occasion he was beaten he finished a good third against older opposition in the Prix de l'Abbaye de Longchamp.

**AR3** 158 I did though on one occasion not long ago, pluck up the courage to attempt the required sort of reply.

**Grammar**

Your query was:
*if I were you*

**ARJ** 3148 I'd walk now if I were you.

**B0U** 2690 I think I should begin to get changed now if I were you.

**CA0** 750 I'd hide that if I were you.

**CAU** 521 Regular readers will know that I have been a fan of Stephen Coonts since I reviewed his first novel Flight of the Intruder (now a major (?) film, as they say, though I'd make do with the book if I were you).

**Colligation**

Your query was:
*by*

**A04** none Distributed under licence by Oxford University Computing Services on behalf of the BNC Consortium.

**A68** 2514 Ramsey, formerly put off by Eden's drawl, was at first put off by Macmillan's blear-eyed appearance and puffy eyes.

**ACX** 314 Save an extra £11.95 by ordering our BBC Gardeners' World Magazine Special Pack, containing Starter Kit and a 50ft Soakerhose pack at just £39.95.

**Colligation**

Your query was:
*for*

**A0N** 2237 But we will speak up for ourselves.

**A68** 1540 He widened the faculty from being Anglican to being for all denominations.

**A6G** 1170 Perhaps the most important evidence adduced for Maxse's radical right outlook is the fact that he tended to lapse into what Richard Hofstadter saw as the chief characteristic of such politics, namely a 'paranoid style'.

**AAE** 515 With the other five games drawn, the unbeaten run is Australia's best for 15 years.

**Register**

Your query was:
*(in) front of the telly*

**F9D** 1731 Work by Peter Collett, an Oxford academic, has shown clearly that what goes on in front of the telly is, in practice, virtually anything.

**CA9** 722 Sal was a couple of years older than me and Pop would spoil us rotten – meals on trays in front of the telly, day trips to Belle Vue fun park or Blackpool – so I was surprised when one week she refused the usual invitation.

**CH2** 5401 SHE'D love a quiet night at home in front of the telly.

**Register**

Your query was:
*(in) front of the TV*

**CH6** 1972 They are staying at home in front of the TV with a bottle of beer and snacks instead.

**ACM** 1321 They are served at seven, on a coffee table in front of the TV.

**CH6** 7358 Many of the prisoners to whom ITN spoke were too scared to talk in front of the TV cameras.

**HH3** 9807 In fact, by the time they reach the age of 18, most children have spent more time in front of the TV set than at school.

***The Company Words Keep*** can be used by you either individually or as part of a group to explore and develop further your own ideas on chunking. If you have had a look at the theory in Part A – or even tried the activities in Part B – fine!

But perhaps you may even find that having a look at the following sections *first*, and checking and formulating your ideas on chunks, could be a good place to start – leading either to the *practical* or to the *theoretical*. Everything is connected!

Here, then, are some suggested activities and short essays – about your future with chunks.

## The sections

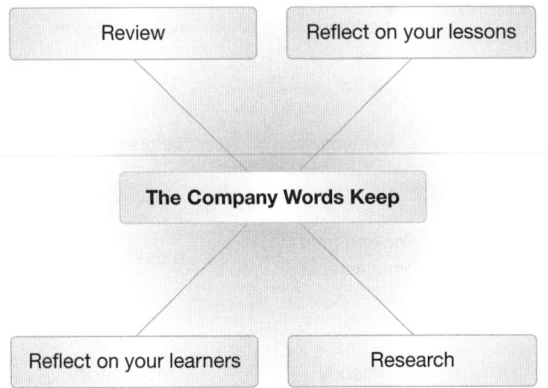

### 1 Review
Background knowledge and terminology.
What do you know about chunking?
Check what you already know or *don't* know about chunks.
Check you have the terminology and the metalanguage needed to talk about or research chunks.

### 2 Reflect on your lessons
Classroom practice.
Consider the chunking syllabus of your coursebook and discover ways to supplement it.
Do some small-scale classroom research on chunking.
Reconcile chunking with correcting and giving helpful feedback to your learners, taking into account the possible interference of their mother tongue.

### 3 Reflect on your learners
Issues with different types of learners.
A discussion of how chunking works with the different age groups you may be working with – children, teenagers and adults.

### 4 Research
A reference list.
An extensive and personal compilation of both the websites and the books that we have found extremely useful.
We hope you will find it helpful – for a fuller understanding of *The Company Words Keep* and for your ongoing development.

# What do you know about chunking?

| | | | | |
|---|---|---|---|---|
| acronym | active listening | alignment | binomials | blended learning |
| BNC simple search | brain sludge | British National Corpus (BNC) | Chomskian competence | chunk |
| cliché | collocation | colligation | concordance | concordancer |
| corpus | Cuisenaire rods | Data Driven Learning (DDL) | deductive/inductive approach | deixis |
| delexification | deterministic/ probabilistic grammar | digital natives | discourse markers | elision |
| ellipsis | enallage | environment | ephemera | filler |
| fixed expression | frequency list | genre | hedging | holding device |
| holophrase | idiolect | incompleteness | key word | language play |
| lexical density | lexicographer | Linguistic Psychodrama | looking after your listener | metalanguage |
| mondegreen | pragmatics | priming | prosody | redundancy |
| retention | retrieval | routines | shared knowledge | Silent Way |
| sketch engine | slot | SMS | textspeak | tolerance of ambiguity |
| twisted cliché | utterance | vagueness | wiki | word partnership |

# Review

## What do you know about chunking?

### If you are working alone:

You may be browsing through *The Company Words Keep* and have only looked briefly at Part A and Part B. Or you may by now have read Part A more closely and used a few, or even a fair number of, the activities from Part B.

Either way, take a look at the terms presented in the grid opposite – How much do you know?

Many of the terms used in the Glossary on page 21 were new to the authors at the time of writing this book.

- If you don't know a term, refer back to the Glossary – they are all presented in full, with definitions.
- If you know the term already, refer back to the Glossary and see if you agree with our definition.

When you have finished, you should now have a rough idea of what you do know and what you don't.

### If you are working with colleagues or in a teacher development group:

There are many ways of checking on your colleagues' or trainees' knowledge. We suggest the following, and have designed this section accordingly:

- Cut up the grid opposite, or a similar one with the terms that you wish to concentrate on.
- Give each member of the group one or two of the terms and a copy of the definitions.
- Ask them to check they know the meaning of the term(s) they have been allocated.
- Get them moving around checking and clarifying each other's terms until they are reasonably confident about the definitions.

You can finish off with a brief plenary discussion.

Probably some of the terms will have struck you and interested you. As an optional extension, you can choose the ones that most intrigued you, browse the book and find an activity which deals with the subject matter of the terms – this will enable you to try this aspect out more in class.

What may happen is that the terms known from 'pre-chunk' methodology surface again with a different slant when talking about the Lexical Approach. A new chunk can be made up of well-known words, such as *immigrant*, *native* and *IT*, yielding new chunks – such as *IT native/IT immigrant* and *digital native/digital immigrant*.

# Reflect on your lessons

## Chunks and the coursebook

### How well does your coursebook teach lexis?

Probably, like most teachers, you have to use a coursebook – because of institutional constraints or because it gives you and your learners a useful, basic syllabus to work from.

However, coursebooks often lack a clear lexical syllabus and need to be adapted and supplemented.

In fact, you wouldn't be looking at resource books like this one if you thought the coursebook offered you and your learners a completely self-contained course. There may be a number of reasons for your concern:

- You may harbour some doubts about how the coursebook you are using actually teaches lexis.
- The coursebook may not offer enough work on lexis.
- The coursebook has a very limited repertoire of lexical activities.
- The way lexis is presented and taught does not seem to bring the expected results and progress.

> 'We go in and I do my thing, and then we supplement it with whatever we want.'
> Caroline Corr, musician

Let's take a more detailed look at this. Take a copy of your coursebook (not forgetting the teacher's book):

- Browse through and assess a few of the places where it deals with lexis.
- Note how often the activities focus on single words, how often on chunks.
- Observe how much learner training and memory training there is for storing and retrieving chunks of language.
- Check how the introduction and the explanations in the teacher's book deal with lexis, and assess how the authors *think* they deal with lexis.

We need to be careful here: a great many coursebooks say they have a full lexical syllabus, often backed up by corpus research. However, in our experience and with very few exceptions, this is a mere bolt-on, rather than any real systematic use of corpus and lexical chunking.

As well as coursebook texts, in our own classes we use texts from other sources to work on lexis and explore or collect chunks. Before reading on, consider the following question:

- Where do the 'texts' teachers use in class come from?

The answer would seem to be: the learner / the teacher / authentic texts / resource books / the Web – as well as, of course, the coursebook itself.

In this book, we have suggested ways of exploiting coursebook texts but, also, we use texts from other sources. Turn back to Part B and skim the activities – you will find the following:

- Activities which use the lexis from the coursebook, but with a twist
- Activities which use text from the teacher
- Activities which use text from the learner
- Activities which use authentic text
- Activities which use text from the Web
- Activities which simply catch your eye (ie a 'resource book' activity)

If you go back and take a look at your coursebook, you can see how these activities can be successfully integrated into the lexical syllabus suggested by the book you are using.

# Reflect on your lessons

## Chunks and classroom research

### Do you want to know more than you know?

There are various models for small-scale classroom research which are well known. Action research, questionnaires and reflective practice are all used for ongoing research, for personal development or to get data for an assignment for a professional teaching qualification when you are in training of some kind. They are all suitable if you want to do some formal or informal research into chunking and the ideas and activities we put forward in this book.

Below, however, we have chosen to outline one of the lesser-known models – a simple 'quota-sampling device'. This is partly because it *is* less well known, but mainly because, in our opinion, it is more rigorous, and so gives better results, than most other research models.

- **Decide on a population.**

This can be simply the learners in your school who are all in class at a chosen level.

- **Decide what you wish to investigate.**

This could be done by having a brief discussion with the class on how they feel about chunking/a lexical approach. Be as non-directive as possible and, in light of the discussion, tighten up your area of enquiry – a general question such as *'Do you think lexis is useful?'* will bring poor results. Learners will respond better to a concrete question such as *'How useful were the worksheets on lexis we did last Tuesday and Thursday?'*

- **Select a small representative sample.**

The sample could be just half a dozen learners who you ask to give up a little of their time. However, they should be representative: If most of the learners are girls, then four girls and two boys should be asked. If most are unmotivated to learn English, then chose a majority who are unmotivated. If half have a laptop, then chose half who have a laptop and half who don't. All types of learners should be represented.

The criteria will obviously vary according to your knowledge of the population you have chosen to sample.

- **Collect data from the sample.**

Get the learners talking, and collect data by making copious notes or recording the conversation. Again, this should be as non-directive as possible, other than to focus the learners on the question in hand. Ideally, this should be done by someone else, rather than you the researcher. It may involve extra effort to enlist the help of a colleague, but having a neutral person collecting the data gives much more rigour to the process, as researchers often get the answers they expect – and research should be done without interference.

- **Examine the data.**

Interpret the data, draw conclusions, review the process and reflect on the results.

The above procedure is relatively simple but it offers an objective way to collect data. The learner quoted at the beginning of this section asked for *'other kinds of stuff'*. There is only one way to find out what that 'stuff' is – by classroom research. Research has three uses:

- It is a way of getting feedback and improving our practice.
- It is part of personal development to improve our teaching and satisfaction.
- It is often a required part of a training programme (eg DELTA/MA dissertation).

If it is done regularly, it can become part of our practice so that, instead of doing it consciously, it becomes an unconscious part of our everyday teaching.

> *'We need other kinds of stuff.'*
> A learner participating in classroom research

We first came across this research method at a session given by Diane Mary Kent at an IATEFL symposium in Slovakia.

# Reflect on your lessons

## Chunks and feedback

### Can feedback be counter-productive?

We need to be aware of how we introduce lexical items, and then how we address the learners' attempts to use them in chunks. When learners pick up a new single lexical item, they translate it into their mother tongue or try to make sense of how to use it in some other way – often with unfortunate results. The teacher plays an important role in the process of how the learner makes the new lexical item their own and useable. Feedback at this point is vital.

Naturally, learners try to use the new item of lexis. Often it is a single word deprived of its typical chunk context. Sometimes learners make good guesses, sometimes not. However, the way the teacher goes about *explaining* the problem may be constructive – or not.

The following two reconstructions are based on true stories, and they show how two teachers can approach, in different ways, going about dealing with learner mischunking. The learner had learned the word 'resounding' and, in their mother tongue, the words 'great' and 'resounding' are to some point interchangeable.

**Scenario 1**

Learner: It was a resounding view.
Teacher: No, you can't say this in English.
Learner: Why?
Teacher: Because we don't say that …
Learner: Ah!

**Scenario 2**

L: It was a resounding view.
T: No, you can't say that. It's not good English …
L: But 'resounding' means 'great'. You said the other day …
T: Yes, but this is not English, this is *in* English.
L: But why? … It's what it means.
T: Well, yes, but you can only say 'resounding success', 'resounding defeat', 'resounding victory'. Failure or success.
L: So you can say 'resounding test result'?
T: Not really.
L: But why? Please explain.
T: Let's look it up on the BNC.

In both situations, the learners tried to use the word 'resounding' in a new L2 language context. Possibly they tried to translate, but they were unable to see the limitations that come with the word and its uses in chunks which are dissimilar to their L1. In the two situations, the learners were learning about the limitations/chunks in which the word appears:

- Situation 1 – the teacher was unhelpful.
- Situation 2 – the teacher initiated a significant discovery process.

The above scenarios are a common-enough experience. A learner has learnt a word in isolation and so, although they have given effort to understanding the meaning, they have no idea which other word(s) it is 'primed' to co-occur with. And it's difficult for them to understand *why* their creative chunking is wrong – which is, after all, reasonable since this is based on custom and practice by the native-speaker community rather than any logic. Learners want to experiment but everywhere are chained to (seemingly) arbitrary rules. The teacher's role is to clarify and offer strategies (like consulting the British National Corpus) to store the L2 chunks which best correspond to the L1 ones.

> *'Every teacher should learn one thing from each lesson.'*
> Caleb Gattegno

# Reflect on your lessons

Another example: in many languages, 'since' and 'for' (referring to duration in time) are both represented by one word. The two confusing English equivalents do not seem logical to learners, who argue with the teacher that *since two days* is acceptable. They often try to prove their point by translating into the mother tongue. They cannot get over the L1 interference: Why is *since two days* wrong?

### The mother tongue – interference or helpful resource?

Translation plays an important role in learning chunks. Skilled translators and interpreters are masters of chunk retrieval. The process goes like this: a chunk in one language provides the stimulus for retrieving a chunk in another. There is not much time wasted, often not much time to think. It could be described as 'linguistic behaviourism'.

In language teaching, we also need to focus on L1 chunks and their correspondence in L2, and vice-versa. No matter what level the learners are, they try to translate, often word for word. Then, at best, they produce utterances that are *in* English – but not *English*. Translation is not a bad thing – but it has to be taught properly. The teacher just needs to make the learners aware that L1 and L2 chunks that have the same meaning may differ a lot.

Take the following examples of chunk translations:

German: *Du wirst auf andere Gedanken kommen.* (Literally: *'You will go to other thoughts.'*)
English: *It will take you out of yourself.*

Italian: *Buona notte!* (Summing up how a car accident happened: *'Good night!'*)
English: *Bingo!*

Raising the learners' awareness of chunk translation may be done through L1 and L2 text comparison. You need to find the right resources and websites to assist this process.

You can research the materials you *can* access in English and in your learners' mother tongue:

- a fragment of a novel
- a poem
- a political speech
- an article
- a DVD film with a 'choose the language' option
- a DVD film with subtitles in one of the two languages
- a song
- a news item
- a play
- an interview

Looking for such materials can be an ongoing process, and you may want to start a special file where you store your sources for chunk translation.

If learners are exposed to the idea of chunking in their mother tongue, then their L1 can be a *resource* to approach L2, rather than an *interference*. The following strategies in the search for helpful feedback can help:

- Prepare examples and activities to show the learners how chunks work in their mother tongue and in the target language.
- Make a list of chunks that are abused by foreigners in the learners' mother tongue or that children often mischunk (often learners have examples of their own or their siblings which have passed into family folklore).
- Find (both you and your learners) examples of mischunking from radio and TV.
- Refer the learners to programmes, articles or letters to the newspaper where language 'experts' pick on common mischunkings or inappropriate usage.

The point is to make the learners *aware* – of priming, and how mischunking can sound in their own language: and so lessen their resistance to accepting it in the target language.

> 'Language is an art, like brewing or baking ... It certainly is not a true instinct, for every language has to be learnt.'
> Charles Darwin

# Reflect on your learners

## Chunks and children

*'Ever tried? Ever failed? Try again. Fail better.'*
Samuel Beckett

### Can we recreate in class the way native speakers learn the language?

Evidence suggests that native children learn their mother tongue by observing, hypothesising and experimenting. They first 'parrot', repeating simple words and phrases they have heard in a social context, then they start to produce their own phrases and sentences, before moving on to longer utterances. The role of chunks is very important in the process, so the way children learn their mother tongue has implications for a language class of young learners.

At the beginning, very small children don't necessarily understand the word or chunk they hear and then try to say. They may not be aware of how many words a given chunk consists of, and may have only a vague idea what it means. They have heard it used in a given situation and try it out to test its limitations and narrow down its use.

If a carer points at a black cat and says 'black', there is no way the child can know the meaning. It could mean *colour* or *name* or *nice* or *soft* or *danger* or *present*. A child's experimentation on the surroundings is necessary, and might go something like this:

Points to ginger cat: *Black*. Notices feedback and thinks: *Black does not mean 'cat'*.
Points to red car: *Black*. Feedback. *No, try again*.
Points to black car: *Black. Mmm. Promising*.
Points to black hair: *Black. Ah-ah*.
Points to black cat: *Black. Right. Got it!*

In a language class, the children learning chunks are older, their language instinct is much better developed and so is their intellect. Also, if need be, the teacher can clarify the meaning by using L1. The accumulation of language is therefore faster but the mechanism is the same:

- First come single words and chunks.
- Then come longer utterances.

Native children at about the age of two first use words and chunks to communicate. They also use single words which have the quasi-status of sentences (these are called 'holophrases'). They quickly progress to stringing more words and chunks together in a meaningful way, which is the first sign of using or following rules. They also learn to use intonation at this stage so that they can make a statement or question or exclamation, depending on what kind of exchange or expression they want to initiate. Grammar comes much later.

In language teaching methodology, this points to more focus on chunks at early stages of learning the language by both children and older learners. The joy of being able to communicate fluently and without mistakes is a great motivator. Grammar can be weaved in gradually.

When native children are three years old, a linguistic breakthrough takes place. They learn faster and may double their vocabulary within six months, from 500 to 1000 words.

In a language class, this kind of progress is unlikely – but it *is* possible in class to focus on contexts in which given chunks can be used by young language learners. Also, we can expand the learners' knowledge of lexis by focusing on various combinations of known words to make up new chunks which use a limited pool of vocabulary. Small children also quickly discover that the same word said with a different intonation has a different meaning. Language learners made aware of intonation and stress in a chunk will also improve how they express themselves in English.

# Reflect on your learners

Many teachers expect their learners to speak fluently, without hesitation and in full sentences, much too soon. Native children at pre-school age have a natural stammer and a seeming lack of fluency. In this period there seems to be a kind of regression, as children pause a lot and stammer. However, linguists claim that it is not the case, just the opposite:

- It is a sign the children are making progress.
- They have now stored enough words and chunks which are waiting to be used.

When children pause, they are trying to retrieve the 'ready to use' or 'pre-fabricated' bits of language stored in their brains. When they don't have the chunk 'ready at hand' – when they cannot retrieve it quickly enough – they have to improvise, make up a chunk or use other linguistic solutions to communicate, such as insistently using the word 'and' as a holding device or by making multiple repetitions.

This means that the child's speech is characterised by mixed pace:

- Fast – when they are retrieving the appropriate chunks.
- Slower – when the neuron pathways are not as well-beaten as an adult's, which slows down the retrieval process.
- Very slow – when they have to improvise, as they haven't retained or are unable to retrieve the chunk they need.

Children are able to express themselves successfully for their age, but are often hard to follow. In a language class, many teachers expect a much more mature delivery from their young learners, not realising that this kind of distorted speech is a natural learning process and a lot of work goes into making it more fluent.

What we need are varied ways of presenting chunks, and even more activities and techniques for their storage and fast retrieval to activate the neuron paths. Also, patience is called for. Speech delivery of naturally mixed pace is a sign of successful storage of some chunks and evidence of problem areas to work on.

Many carers of native children have a very positive attitude towards any language the children produce. First, they do not correct, or hardly ever, and are happy with whatever language the child has produced. Carers grade down their own language for the child and are willing to playfully repeat any utterance the child has produced over and over. Only later do they begin to pick up on grammatical and lexical mistakes, often focusing on form rather than meaning.

In a language class, teachers may put emphasis on accuracy and well-rounded delivery at too early a stage. Also, error correction needs to be gradual and constructive.

Sometimes you can hear opinions that in class the teacher is the only source of language, whereas in the mother-tongue environment children learn a lot from each other and give each other a lot of language practice. In class, the latter can *also* take place, especially with regard to chunks, as once a chunk has been stored correctly by a learner it can then be retrieved and taught to peers.

Chunking, as a natural process of retrieval, is therefore especially relevant to children and younger learners, who seem to learn primarily by hypothesis and experiment. By subordinating grammar to lexis in the early stages, we will encourage children and young learners to be more confident and fluent and mirror natural learning processes.

We have given a brief outline of how children learn their mother tongue. There are significant implications for ELT in general, and teaching young learners in particular, which

# Reflect on your learners

are addressed in the questions below and proposed as subjects for reflection:

- What do you tend to focus on more: single words or chunks?
- If a learner uses the wrong chunk, how do you react? Should you just praise any attempt? Do you correct? If so, at what age?
- Do you insist on the children using full sentences?
- Do you offer enough opportunity for the learners to clarify the use of chunks?
- Do you offer enough exposure for the learners to observe language and hypothesise?
- How much do you insist that the children imitate the model you present?
- What is the balance and importance of 'grammar vs lexis' in your lessons? Do you teach lexis then grammar, or grammar then lexis?
- Do you rush children when you expect them to produce language?
- Is the acquisition period long enough?
- Do you avoid the use of metalanguage?
- Do you appreciate the creative use of the language?
- Do you 'play around' and use puns enough?

Observing how native children learn their mother tongue is inspiring for English teachers of young learners, as well those who teach older ones. There is no doubt that chunks are the building blocks of language which are stored in the brain waiting to be used. They need to be retrieved in a fraction of a second and strung together with other chunks, with grammar weaved around them. If we take these reflections on board, our learners will learn more successfully.

## Chunks and teenagers

### Is a change of strategy in order?

Donald Rumsfeld's statement was greeted with hilarity (look up 'known unknowns' on YouTube to see him in action). But he has a point, not in what he says but in what he does *not* say: he does *not* mention the 'unknown knowns' – which are of interest to us here with regard to chunks of language and the teenager.

Teachers teach what they know their learners don't know. In other words, they focus on the 'known unknowns'. Maybe, with teenagers, it's worth adding a strategy and bringing to the surface the 'unknown knowns'. To quote Caleb Gattegno (from a lecture we attended):

*'Every learner knows much more than they think they know. Every learner knows much, much more than the teacher thinks they know.'*

A teenager who is beginning to learn English or who is starting again at an elementary level in a new secondary school knows a lot of chunks that are not usually utilised, and their presence in the learners' brains is not recognised in the class.

The deposits of such wasted and unused information are called 'brain sludge'. If we can bring this brain sludge to light, it can speed up the learning process, anchor new chunks to the unconsciously remembered ones, provide a firm basis for further progress through learner independence and, last but not least, boost confidence.

This last point is important, as psychologists point out that a lot of teenagers' frustration results from the fact that they are always made aware of what they don't know and that they are aware of an external sense of control – while what they want is to take the initiative into their own hands.

> '... we know there are known knowns; there are things we know we know. We also know there are known unknowns; that is to say we know there are some things we do not know. But there are also unknown unknowns – the ones we don't know we don't know.'
> Donald Rumsfeld
> (George W Bush's defence secretary)

# Reflect on your learners

Where does brain sludge come from? Teenagers are now exposed to more and more English in their environment and across the various media, and they are learning English constantly even when, or especially when, they are not aware of it. Learners often know sophisticated chunks, even when they don't know basic ones with the same key word, as in this exchange with a (low-level) learner:

Learner: *Can I have a …?* (the learner doesn't know 'paper tissue')
Teacher: *… paper tissue.*
Learner: *What is scar tissue?*
Teacher: *Why are you asking?*
Learner: *It's in a song.*

It is a shame to waste the potential of such a resource. Also, we need to reconcile the English encountered in class with the English the learners encounter outside class. In class, the learners are rarely in charge of the language they learn. When they leave, they take control of the language they learn and can be made aware of the English that surrounds them. If we focus their attention on such chunks, they will be absorbing language they can then use in and outside the class. Let's follow some possible sources you may want to explore.

## Songs

Teenagers encounter in songs lots of lexical chunks (*Erase and rewind*, The Cardigans – the examples we give are from the recesses of our minds!), grammatical chunks (*Wish you were here*, Pink Floyd), 'mondegreens' (*Kiss this guy/kiss the sky*, Jimi Hendrix) and 'enallage' (*Is you is or is you ain't my baby?* Louis Jordan). Any group of young people will come up with their own, which tend to be specific to age, gender and 'now'; they will be very different from what the teacher knows. Researching a word and how it appears in song chunks is a pathway into the teenage brain sludge (see www.urbandictionary, a wiki-dictionary by teens for teens).

## The environment

We are being more and more exposed to English in our environment, even when we don't live in an English-speaking country. We can explore the following:

**Packaging** Any room in any house will have brand names and packaging using English: *Pedigree Chum*, *Vanish Oxi-Action Gel*, *Fruit of the Loom*, and many many more.

**Notices and information** Lots of English is used in international places such as airports and tourist sites: *Push to open*, *Authorised staff only*, *Gate open*, and so on.

**Advertisements** Many adverts on the street and in the media have their slogans and punch lines in English as well as the local language: *I'm lovin' it*, *Just do it*, *The future is bright, the future is Orange*. When we were writing this section for the book, we needed some examples of advertising slogans. We googled 'famous slogans' and found:

http://www.buzzle.com/articles/famous-advertising-slogans.html
http://www.famousquotes.me.uk/slogans/famous-slogan-46.htm

New to us! It just shows: it's all there – if you look.

**Technology** Even when the software is translated into the local language, there are still a great many English chunks (although they are often pronounced in the local way). *Cut and paste*, *Delete all*, *Times New Roman* on computers; *SMS*, *EMS*, *Withheld* on mobiles. There are many instructions and lexical sets in computer games, too – we were given a detailed explanation of the difference between a *ghoul* and a *ghost* by one elementary learner. Why not ask the learners to switch their mobile phone language to English?

# Reflect on your learners

Mobiles, Twitter and email obviously have specific genres, and how one expresses oneself takes on a different form when using them. The research seems to show that teenagers have a sophisticated view of genre, and know full well that what is acceptable in the genre of 'text speak' is not acceptable in formal letters, etc – at least in their L1. It may be that they misjudge what is acceptable in L2, so there is an opportunity for the teacher to clarify.

However, research at Cambridge University has shown that the more skilled the teenager is at text messaging, the better they are at recognising the appropriate language to use in everyday situations and in a 'restricted use' situation – an exam task, for example. As we have noted elsewhere in this book, it is often the learners who are 'natives' in the area of new technology (we, the authors, will be forever non-natives in this area). Exploiting new technology can be a real confidence booster for learners who have the skills and competence, providing the teacher does not feel de-skilled!

**The Web** This is an obvious source – and very wide! It is unlikely that any teenager who uses the Web to access the things they are interested in can do so without encountering huge amounts of English language. It is interesting to note that the English is not always correct or authentic, and can be non-native or any variety, so the teacher's role here is exploring and clarifying. For example: What is American usage and what is British? What is formal and what is colloquial? What is written and what is spoken? The ARC model proposed by Jim Scrivener is helpful here – see page 20 in Part A.

**Inclusive culture** Teenagers have their own culture which is meant to be 'exclusive'. They will share it with teachers sometimes and the teacher will be given a chance to learn – from the learner. One of our own learners gave us the poems by Tupac Shakur. In our opinion his poetry, if published by a small obscure imprint, would win the Nobel prize for literature (check it on the Web). But because he was a rap artist who was gunned down by his rivals, it is largely kept in the realm of teen culture.

We have outlined the areas of interest. Since they are there sloshing around in teenagers' heads as 'unknown knowns', we need to bring them to the surface, recognise and explore them in a respectful way. This suggests the following:

- More emphasis on learner autonomy
- The use of text that the learners themselves know or can collect
- The teacher's role of clarifying and categorising the text, together with the learners
- The use of Web resources created by teenagers (such as *urbandictionary*) or frequented by teenagers (such as YouTube or lyrics sites)
- The use of the Web for homework and research by the teenagers
- Letting *them* look for language as well as 'giving' it to them

You can start with the places to research language given above, then find out from the learners what could be a likely source: Role Playing Games, computer games, etc. A case in point: recently in class we heard the following exchange:

Learner 1: (to teacher) *What's the difference between these words?*
Learner 2: (to learner 1) *Look it up in the BNC.*

Teens now know more than they used to know because of the internationalisation of English and the Web and other media, which builds up their confidence and motivation. They are exposed to lots of authentic use which they absorb naturally. Exploring this knowledge in class will also help the process of clarifying which chunks of language are suitable, and when they can be used.

# Reflect on your learners

## Chunks and adults

### Teaching for life?

Adult learners are diverse, and some of the points made in the previous sections regarding children and teenagers learning chunks of language also apply to adults. Some may learn the chunks the way small children do, ie by observing, hypothesising and experimenting.

A plumber may want to learn English to work in Ireland or a waiter to get a job in an international restaurant on better pay. They are clever enough to realise that the English class will be to their advantage but they are not be interested in, or necessarily comfortable with, a traditional classroom set-up. Lexical chunking lends itself to a course in survival English, or the practical language needed for plumbing or 'waiting table' in a restaurant.

Another category who will benefit from a more non-academic course based on survival English and lexical chunks are those adult leisure learners (often older or retired) who see English as a useful hobby and want it for holiday travel. Again, the practicality and different approach that lexical chunking offers will appeal.

The plumbers, the waiting staff or the retired hobbyist will probably have already picked up some chunks from the environment, as they have real-world experience and motivations. What we can do is help them notice more and sensitise them to the chunks they need in a more systematic way. This will also apply to more academic learners who need specialised chunks for their study or for their profession.

Adult learners may be beginners learning English in a class. However, they may have already learned one or more other foreign languages. They may transfer some of their bad habits regarding learning lexis from their past experiences. By bad habits we mean learning single words, words out of context, colourful idioms which are rarely used, etc. The teacher is therefore responsible for good habit formation from the very beginning.

Adult learners may have learned general English as teenagers, but now need to do more specialised courses because they have to use English in a professional environment. Or learners at universities have to come to terms with academic discourse and jargon, as some courses at their universities may be delivered in English. Familiarisation with lexical chunks will obviously be a massive help in their use of language in a specific professional context.

Strategies need to be developed for observing and retaining the chunks relevant to their chosen area. What is desirable here is a kind of 'linguistic mimicry' of best practice. A businessperson who attends a business English course will pick up a lot of useful language, but in addition they may learn much more from playing with chunks online. Have a look at:

*http://www.businessbuzzwordbingo.com/*
*http://www.lovelyjane.btinternet.co.uk/bullshit.htm*

It's amazing how many chunks found on the above websites are absent from the average 'English for business' coursebook. Writers do not have access to confidential business meetings. So the adult English learner who is a businessperson will have to go into a meeting and absorb the language chunks – picking them up as they go along. If they are used to chunks in class, they will find this easier.

Take an adult learner who is a practising doctor and uses English at the hospital. They will have to pick up sets of equivalent chunks: official medical chunks for medical records and the colloquial chunks the patients are likely to use, for example: *femur* vs *thighbone*, *urinate* vs *pass water*, *bowel movement* vs *number two*. Additionally, they may have to learn a third set of Latin chunks (as pronounced in English, not as pronounced in their mother tongue).

> 'Education is the best provision for the journey to old age.'
> Aristotle

# Reflect on your learners

A lawyer who is aware of the BNC Law corpus and knows how to access it may want to know more about the chunks containing, say, the word 'jury'. They can look up a concordancer website and get the data.

It is not infrequent, then, that adult learners of English want lexical outcomes from a language class that can be directly applied in their professional lives. It may be to do with the fact that they do not have much time and are under 'language pressure' at work. In our experience, students of physiotherapy whose English is relatively low-level don't want to learn only general English, they also want to see how what they learn can be applied in their future work. The grammar and functions of a general English course are easily transferable. What they need are the *chunks* that will help them with the transfer from general to physiotherapy English.

Adult learners will soon leave the language class, for any number of reasons, and will have to continue learning on their own. Good habit formation regarding learning chunks is part of lifelong learning and continuing education. Learners will have to keep learning chunks – not only because they progress professionally or branch out, but also because the language is changing all the time and they will need to learn new lexis, keeping track of how their discipline develops. Learning to learn chunks as an adult is a professional must.

Thinking about answers to the questions below may help you to view the issues from a new perspective:

- How often do you consider the reasons why your adult learners are learning English?
- How do you find out about their motivation?
- Do you take on board their reasons for learning English and address their needs?
- Are you able to classify your learners as EFL, ESL, EIL, EAP, ESP, etc?
- Are you aware in what scenarios they use or will need to use English outside class?
- Do your learners get from you enough tools and techniques to become independent learners?
- How do you use specialised dictionaries with your learners?
- Do you teach them single words or the chunks they need, or both?
- Do you direct them to the right sources to follow up queries and research language chunks?
- Do you learn new chunks together with your learners in an investigative and cooperative way?

More than any other group, adult learners are likely to see the benefits of learning the chunks of their specialism and, indeed, may already know more than the teacher! This suggests that the teacher needs to cooperate rather than be the expert 'knower', and that a facilitative research-based way of teaching is especially appropriate. The aim is to create an independent learner who can continue to notice and use chunks in their professional or work environment.

# Research

## The Web

> *'When in doubt go to the data.'*
> J R Firth

The internet can be very helpful in researching chunks in general. It is particularly useful:

- for teachers who want to check their intuition;
- for teachers who are unsure about the exact wording of a chunk;
- for those learners who would like to research language by themselves.

In this section, we would like to categorise and characterise some of the useful and inspiring websites or tools we can find on the Web. Many of these are already referenced at point-of-need elsewhere in the book – for use in specific activities. Here, they are grouped according to their features. The list is by no means exhaustive: its aim is to support a more lexical approach to our teaching, as suggested throughout *The Company Words Keep*.

### Corpus websites

The corpus websites below can provide us with the environment of a word, the frequency of a word or chunk, and the source. They provide us with 'data to interpret', rather than 'expert opinion'. Using the data from the websites suggests a methodological shift as the teacher is not the arbiter. It calls for a more cooperative approach, in which teachers investigate with the learners and draw conclusions from the available evidence.

First, a website that gives a very straightforward introduction to the corpus and its uses to compile dictionaries: *www.askoxford.com*.

The British National Corpus (BNC) at *http://sara.natcorp.ox.ac.uk/lookup.html* is also a good introduction to the corpus. Click on 'Simple search', type in a word or chunk – and it will list up to 50 random example sentences in which the item is used. Click on the left-hand icon at the beginning of each example – and you access the source of the sentence. Each time you look up examples, a different set of sentences will appear – so copy and save them in a Word file if you want to use some specific examples in a lesson.

A very user-friendly website which enables a comparison between the spoken and the written corpus of the BNC is: *http://corpus.byu.edu/bnc*. It is free to subscribe.

You can also access various corpora through concordancer tools, for example at: *http://www.lextutor.ca/concordancers/concord_e.html*. You can specify areas of interest to you including Spoken Language, Legal English and Medical English. In each case, you see the selected word used in a chunk.

For more advanced work on word partnerships, there are more sophisticated tools such as: *www.sketchengine.co.uk*.

Visual learners will enjoy the visual thesaurus at: *http://www.wordsift.com/visualize*, part of the Wordsift website, or the Visual Word Partnership Dictionary and Thesaurus at: *http://www.visuwords.com/*.

Recent developments are: English Profile, which presents the language learners' corpus at various levels at: *http://www.englishprofile.org/*; and corpora of English as it is spoken by non-native speakers in different contexts, eg VOICE (Vienna-Oxford International Corpus of English) at: *http://www.univie.ac.at/voice/*.

### The Web as a corpus

**Google** The whole Web is a giant international corpus in itself. You can look up many language queries but they are not specific to a given variety of English (eg British English vs American English) – more like English as a Lingua Franca.

# Research

**Research** You can type a language chunk into Google, eg 'international summit', and obtain endless examples of how the chunk is used. You can choose a corpus that you wish to research at: *http://www.webcorp.org.uk/*. If you would like to investigate, for example, various options of the chunk *I would like to welcome you*, simply type into Google the phrase followed by *, and you obtain data to research language.

**Visuals** If you go into Google Images and type in the word 'house', you will then get many pictures of houses with captions in chunks such as: *White House, our house plans, historical museum house, house of the future*, etc.

**Comparison** The following site uses Google, adapting it as a giant corpus and enabling the comparison of two chunks: *http://corpus.byu.edu/bnc*.

**Games** You can also research word frequencies in a fun way at: *www.googlefight.com*. When you type in two words or chunks you want to compare, two stickpeople have a fight and you get the frequency result in bar graph form.

## Web tools

There are many Google tools that focus on single words, and we need to look for ways to use them to research chunks.

**Online dictionaries** No further description needed. Here are some examples:
*http://www.urbandictionary.com/define.php?term=online*
*http://acronyms.thefreedictionary.com/PC&QT*
*http://www.macmillandictionary.com/*

**Frequency lists** Lists of the 20/50/100/500 most common words in English are easily downloadable (or can be found in books and CD-ROMs). The lists vary slightly according to the source; however, for ELT purposes, the differences are insignificant. To look for them, simply type into the search engine 'most common words' or 'most common words in English', or go directly to: *http://en.wikipedia.org/wiki/Most_common_words_in_English*
*http://www.duboislc.org/EducationWatch/First100Words.html*

**Vocabprofile** A tool that divides words in a text according to four categories, also taking frequencies into consideration: *http://www.lextutor.ca/vp/eng/*

**Visual representation** Programs that analyse a text and highlight the most common words: *http://www.wordle.net/* and *http://www.wordsift.com/*

**Frequency games** You can play at: *http://www.sporcle.com/games/common_english_words.php*

**Specialised word lists** Compilations for academic purposes, for example at:
*http://www.nottingham.ac.uk/~alzsh3/acvocab/*

## Authentic texts

The Web offers a lot of authentic texts which are ideal for working on chunks.

**Mondegreens** *http://www.kissthisguy.com/*

**Language overheard** *http://www.overheardinlondon.co.uk*
*http://www.overheardinnewyork.com*

**Film scripts** *http://dir.yahoo.com/entertainment/movies_and_film/screenplays/*
*http://www.simplyscripts.com/* and *http://www.awesomefilm.com/*

**Extreme authenticity** *www.foundmagazine.com* and *www.engrish.com*

**Others** *http://www.bbc.co.uk/worldservice/learningenglish/language/wordsinthenews/*
*www.bullshitbingo.net*

# Research

## Bibliography

> *'Worldly wisdom teaches us that it is better for reputation to fail conventionally than to succeed unconventionally.'*
> John Maynard Keynes

Many of the books in this Bibliography were ignored or neglected when they were first published.

This limited bibliography is necessarily biased to our investigation of lexical chunking, developed over time.

### Chunks and language corpora

J R Firth did the basic groundwork on colligation and collocation in the first half of the twentieth century, and seems to be the grandfather of our thinking about chunks.
See *Papers in Linguistics 1934–1951*, Oxford University Press 1957.

George A Miller, who wrote one of the most highly-cited papers in psychology, 'The Magical Number Seven, Plus or Minus Two', *Psychological Review* 63 (2) 1956, gave neuropsychological insight into the maximum size of a chunk the brain can store.

Around 1990, Jane and Dave Willis joined the staff of Birmingham University, UK, to work on the COBUILD project. They were the authors of *The Collins Cobuild English Course* (a task-based course with a lexical syllabus), a truly corpus and chunk-based course.

The basic academic texts that stressed the importance of lexical chunking were:
*Patterns of Lexis in Text* M Hoey, OUP 1991
*Lexical Phrases in Language Teaching* J R Nattinger and J S DeCarrico, OUP 1992
*Corpus, Concordance, Collocation* J Sinclair, OUP 1991

This was popularised as a method in:
*The Lexical Approach* M Lewis, LTP 1993
'Revising Priorities: from grammatical failure to collocational success' J Hill in *Teaching Collocation* M Lewis (Ed), LTP 2000

Our favourite relatively recent addition to the academic literature is:
*Lexical Priming* M Hoey, Routledge 2005

### Dictionaries

The reference books and the rationale behind them that we have found most useful are:
*Macmillan English Dictionary (MED) – New Edition*, Macmillan 2007
*MED for Advanced Learners – New Edition Teacher's Resource Book*, Macmillan 2007
*Oxford Collocations Dictionary for Students*, OUP 2002

### Spoken grammar

A more lexical approach and an interest in computational linguistics lead us into teaching spoken grammar. This is touched upon (implicitly or explicitly) in some of the activities in this book. Useful references are:
*Grammar of Speech* D Brazil, OUP 1995
*Exploring Spoken English* R Carter and M McCarthy, CUP 1997
*Cambridge Grammar of English* R Carter and M McCarthy, CUP 2006
*English Grammar Today* R Carter, M McCarthy, G Mark and A O'Keeffe, Cambridge 2011
*Politeness* M Brown and P Levinson, CUP 1978
*Vague Language* J Channell, OUP 1994

A fundamental question that is seldom asked is: Why do we speak? The evolution of language in humans is dealt with in:
*Grooming, Gossip and the Origins of Language* R Dunbar, Faber and Faber 1996
*The Human Story* also by Robin Dunbar, Faber and Faber 2004
*Africa: A Biography of a Continent* J Reader, Knopf 1997

# Research

### Children

A useful book on how children learn L1 is:
*Listen to your Child* by David Crystal, Penguin 1986

### Other useful books

*Academic Vocabulary in Use* M McCarthy and F O'Dell, CUP 2008
*Advanced Language Practice* M Vince, Macmillan 2003
*Advanced Learners* A Maley, OUP 2009
*Dictionaries* J Wright, OUP 1999
*From Corpus to the Classroom* A O'Keeffe, M McCarthy and R Carter, CUP 2007
*Grammar* S Thornbury, OUP 2006
*Grammar and Vocabulary for Cambridge Advanced and Proficiency* R Side and G Wellman, Cambridge 1999
*Longman Grammar of Spoken and Written English*, Longman 1999
*Longman Student Grammar of Spoken and Written English* D Biber, S Conrad and G Leech, Longman 2002
*The Internet* S Windeatt et al, OUP 2000
*Vocabulary, Second Edition* J Morgan and M Rinvolucri, OUP 2004

### Paul and Hania

The ideas in this book are inevitably developed in part from earlier works by the authors which may be of interest:
*Dictation* P Davis and M Rinvolucri, CUP 1988
*The Confidence Book* P Davis and M Rinvolucri, Longman 1990
*Learner-based Teaching* C Campbell and H Kryszewska, OUP 1992
*Towards Teaching* C Campbell and H Kryszewska, Heinemann 1995
*Ways of Doing* P Davis, B Garside and M Rinvolucri, CUP 1995
*More Grammar Games* M Rinvolucri and P Davis, CUP 1998

More ideas on lexical chunking by the authors and others can be found online in Humanising Language Teaching Magazine: *http://www.hltmag.co.uk*.

### Discovery and development

▶ New publications and new websites and tools appear – and old favourites disappear. It is important to monitor how new additions and innovations can be used to promote a more lexical approach to learning and teaching.

▶ Once you are hooked on using the Web for chunking, you will discover more and more resources and tools which are worth using, exploring and sharing – as part of your ongoing personal and professional teacher development.

# From the editors

*The Company Words Keep* is written by two authors who have been involved in the study and the teaching of chunks for many years.

Hania Kryszewska is a non-native teacher who understands the situation of many teachers around the world who aren't always sure what word partnerships are *likely* and *unlikely*.

Paul Davis is a native speaker who represents teachers who still want more point-of-need *confidence* in their teaching of lexical chunks, and who might also be unsure of some of the *key terms* in understanding a more lexical approach.

The ideal combination.

- The authors provide the answer to three key questions: What is a chunk? How fixed is a chunk? How long is a chunk?
- They draw from three fundamental factors: the use of corpus data; an increased interest by linguists in word partnerships; and the availability of computational tools that can sort the data with ease and show the environment and the frequency of a word.
- They include a glossary of essential terms: ranging from collocation to colligation, priming to pragmatics, language play to lexical density.

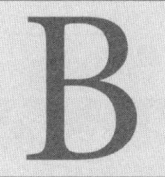

- Five chapters offer a battery of over a hundred techniques and activities that will get your learners chunking.
- The chapters look at introducing and practising chunks, exploiting both the coursebook and authentic texts, as well as making the most of the immense possibilities afforded by the use of Web resources.

- For teachers who want to know more, to reflect on your knowledge of lexical chunks and understand more about the reality of chunking – and perhaps take the steps to find out more for yourselves – *The Company Words Keep* encourages you to undertake further research in the interests of your professional development.
- Nine sections help you to review, reflect and research your knowledge of a more lexical approach.

More than simply compiling a bank of activities, the authors have considered all aspects of using and teaching chunks, from beginners to advanced learners, from the area of ESP to exam preparation. They have moved towards a new methodology: a practical theory of language, of learning – and of teaching.

The ideal solution.

**Mike Burghall**
**Lindsay Clandfield**

# From the publisher

## DELTA TEACHER DEVELOPMENT SERIES

A pioneering new series of books for English Language Teachers
with professional development in mind.

**The Company Words Keep**
by Paul Davis and
Hanna Kryszewska
ISBN 978-1-905085-20-0

**Digital Play**
by Kyle Mawer and
Graham Stanley
ISBN 978-1-905085-55-2

**Teaching Online**
by Nicky Hockly with
Lindsay Clandfield
ISBN 978-1-905085-35-4

**Teaching Unplugged**
by Luke Meddings and
Scott Thornbury
ISBN 978-1-905085-19-4

**The Business English Teacher**
by Debbie Barton,
Jennifer Burkart and
Caireen Sever
ISBN 978-1-905085-34-7

**Culture in our Classrooms**
by Gill Johnson and
Mario Rinvolucri
ISBN 978-1-905085-21-7

**The Developing Teacher**
by Duncan Foord
ISBN 978-1-905085-22-4

**Being Creative**
by Chaz Pugliese
ISBN 978-1-905085-33-0

For details of these and future titles in the series,
please contact the publisher: E-mail info@deltapublishing.co.uk
Or visit the DTDS website at www.deltapublishing.co.uk/titles/methodology